SOCIAL SECURITY AND MEDICARE: MAXIMIZING RETIREMENT BENEFITS

BY THEODORE J. SARENSKI, CPA.PFS, CFP™

Notice to readers

Social Security and Medicare: Maximizing Retirement Benefits is intended solely for use in continuing professional education and not as a reference. It does not represent an official position of the American Institute of Certified Public Accountants, and it is distributed with the understanding that the author and publisher are not rendering legal, accounting, or other professional services in the publication. This course is intended to be an overview of the topics discussed within, and the author has made every attempt to verify the completeness and accuracy of the information herein. However, neither the author nor publisher can guarantee the applicability of the information found herein. If legal advice or other expert assistance is required, the services of a competent professional should be sought.

**You can qualify to earn free CPE through our pilot testing program.
If interested, please visit https://aicpacompliance.polldaddy.com/s/pilot-testing-survey.**

ISBN 978-1-119-73725-4 (paper)
ISBN 978-1-119-73734-6 (ePDF)
ISBN 978-1-119-73733-9 (ePub)
ISBN 978-1-119-73735-3 (obk)

Course Code: **745614**
CL4SSM GS-0419-0A
Revised: **April 2019**

V10018913_060820

Table of Contents

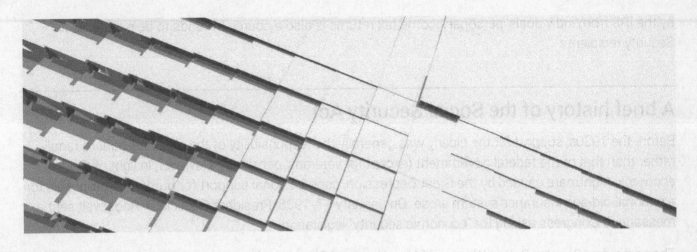

Chapter 1

How the Social Security System Operates

Learning objectives

- Recall that the Federal Insurance Contributions Act (FICA) tax applies to the funding of Social Security retirement, disability benefits, and Medicare benefits.

- Recognize how the additional Medicare tax operates.

- Identify instances in which there is no requirement for FICA taxation.

Overview

On August 14, 1935, the Social Security Act established a delivery system to provide old-age benefits for eligible workers, assistance for victims of industrial accidents, unemployment insurance benefits, and aid for dependent mothers and children, the blind, and the physically handicapped.

In 2016, the Social Security Administration (SSA) paid more than $1 trillion to more than 62 million recipients; 75% were retired workers and their dependents, 16% were disabled workers and their dependents, and 9% were survivors of deceased workers.

The Social Security Act authorized the Social Security Board, which now operates as the Social Security Administration, to register citizens for benefits, administer the contributions received by the federal government, and send payments to recipients. U.S. Social Security "insurance" is supported from "contributions" in the form of taxes on individuals' wages and employers' payrolls rather than directly from government funds. Tax revenue generated from the income tax on Social Security benefits received by the IRS from individuals' personal income tax returns is also a source of funds to be paid to Social Security recipients.

A brief history of the Social Security Act

Before the 1930s, support for the elderly was generally the responsibility of the older individual's family rather than that of the federal government (except for veterans' pensions). However, in light of the economic nightmare caused by the Great Depression, congressional support for numerous proposals for a national old-age insurance system arose. On January 17, 1935, President Franklin D. Roosevelt sent a message to Congress asking for "economic security" legislation.

The same day, Senator Robert Wagner of New York and Representative David Lewis of Maryland introduced bills reflecting the Roosevelt administration's wishes. The resulting Senate and House bills encountered opposition from those who considered it a governmental takeover of individual choice and from those who sought exemption from payroll taxes for employers who adopted government-approved pension plans. Eventually the bill passed both houses, and on August 14, 1935, President Roosevelt signed the Social Security Act into law. Originally, the Social Security Act of 1935 was named the Economic Security Act, but this title was changed during a Ways and Means Committee meeting on March 1, 1935. Congressman Frank Buck (D-Calif.) made a motion to change the name of the bill to the "Social Security Act of 1935." The motion was carried by a voice vote of the committee.

Through the 80th anniversary of Social Security in the year 2015, the Social Security Act has had 12 major legislative changes. The changes have mostly added more workers subject to withholding of Social Security tax on wages, increased the age of eligibility, adjusted the amount of wages subject to Social Security withholding, and other changes meant to shore up what was a shortage of Social Security tax collections at various times in history.

The Bipartisan Budget Act of 2015 passed in November of 2015 rescinded two favorite methods of collecting Social Security benefits: the file and suspend and the restricted application for spousal benefits only at full retirement age (FRA). The two methods were first introduced in the Senior Citizens' Freedom to Work Act of 2000.

File and suspend was a strategy that allowed a worker to file for Social Security benefits at full retirement age and then immediately suspend receiving those benefits to a later age up to age 70. The filing part allowed a spouse or qualifying child to start receiving Social Security benefits on that worker's record even though the worker was delaying their own benefit. File and suspend is still allowed for those workers who were 66 by April 30, 2016. After that date, a spouse or qualifying child will only be allowed to collect a benefit on a worker's record if that worker is actually collecting a benefit. Suspension of benefit collection is still available, meaning that a Social Security recipient between the ages of 62 and 70 can suspend collection of benefits and get additional credits from that moment to age 70. However, as of April 30, 2016, spousal and dependent benefits of that worker are also suspended.

Restricted application is a strategy that became popular after being introduced in the Senior Citizens' Freedom to Work Act. It allowed a spouse at full retirement age to elect to collect only a spousal benefit on their spouse's work record and defer the collecting of his or her own benefit to age 70, collecting an 8% per year credit to their own benefit. People born in 1953 and earlier will still be allowed to file a restricted application. Those people born after 1953 will get the higher of their own benefit or the spousal benefit when they file for Social Security benefit no matter what age they file for the benefit. Therefore, restricted application is still available for those turning age 66 for the next two years.

Lump sum was also eliminated in the Bipartisan Budget Act. The lump sum allowed a person to file and suspend at full retirement age and then at a later age, before age 70, change their mind and collect a lump sum benefit for all of the benefits they would have started receiving at full retirement age to their current age, and also get a monthly benefit starting immediately as if they had begun collecting benefits from full retirement age. The lump sum is only allowed for people who were age 66 by April 30, 2016.

Knowledge check

1. Which began in 1935?

    a. Social Security.
    b. Medicaid.
    c. SSI.
    d. Medicare.

The Social Security Administration

In 1953, the SSA was placed under the Department of Health, Education, and Welfare, which became the Department of Health and Human Services in 1980. In 1994, President Bill Clinton signed 42 USC Section 901 returning the SSA to the status of an independent agency in the executive branch of government.

FICA tax

Social Security's Old-Age, Survivors, and Disability Insurance (OASDI) program and Medicare's Hospital Insurance (HI) program are financed primarily by employment taxes.

Social Security payroll taxes are collected under the authority of the FICA.

The payroll taxes collected for Social Security function as contributions to the social insurance system, commonly known as Social Security. Essentially, FICA operates as the tax provision of the Social Security Act as it appears in the IRC.

Individuals generally never stop paying Social Security and Medicare taxes on work or self-employment earnings, regardless of their age or whether they concurrently receive benefits. Employers continue to be responsible for the matching portion of Social Security and Medicare taxes.

Tax rates are set by law (see Compilation of Social Security Laws at https://www.ssa.gov/OP_Home/comp2/F083-591.html) and apply to earnings up to a maximum amount (https://www.ssa.gov/OACT/COLA/cbb.html#Series) for OASDI (https://www.ssa.gov/OACT/ProgData/taxRates.html).

FICA tax includes two separate taxes. One is Social Security tax and the other is Medicare tax. Different rates apply for each of these taxes.

The current tax rate for Social Security is 6.2% for the employer and 6.2% for the employee, or 12.4% total. The current rate for Medicare is 1.45% for the employer and 1.45% for the employee, or 2.9% total.

Only the Social Security tax has a wage base limit. The wage base limit is the maximum wage that is subject to the tax for that year. For earnings in 2019, this base is $132,900.

There is no wage base limit for Medicare tax. All covered wages are subject to Medicare tax.

Base rates for FICA and Medicare tax rates have not changed and a 0.9% Medicare tax on earned income applies to certain upper-income taxpayers.

FICA and Medicare tax rates

In tax year 2019, the rate is 7.65% in total: 6.2% for the Social Security portion and 1.45% for Medicare.

Beginning January 1, 2013, Additional Medicare Tax applies to an individual's Medicare wages that exceed a threshold amount, based on the taxpayer's filing status. Employers are responsible for withholding the 0.9% Additional Medicare Tax on earned income in excess of $200,000 in a calendar year, without regard to filing status. An employer is required to begin withholding Additional Medicare Tax in the pay period in which it pays wages in excess of $200,000 to an employee and continue to withhold it each pay period until the end of the calendar year. There is no employer match for Additional Medicare Tax.

The taxable wage base

For 2019, the first $132,900 of wages is taxed at 6.2 percent for the non-Medicare element of Social Security. Earnings greater than this amount are taxed for Medicare purposes but not in terms of Social Security retirement, survivor, or disability insurance benefits. Therefore, an employee's maximum Social Security contribution for 2019 is $8,638.50 and for 2018 was $7,979.40 overpayment of Social Security taxes.

Taxpayers who work for more than one employer in any tax year and have earnings in excess of $132,900 in 2019 and $128,700 in 2018 may have paid too much Social Security tax. Keep in mind that when an individual works more than one job in a calendar year, each employer is required to withhold Social Security taxes on wages up to the taxable wage base.

Therefore, a taxpayer may wind up exceeding the maximum Social Security contribution limit. Individuals can claim a tax credit for this overpayment on Form 1040 when they file their personal income tax returns. The excess Social Security tax is shown as an additional payment in the payment section of Form 1040 on page 2.

Knowledge check

2. What does the taxable wage base operate to limit?

    a. The Medicare portion of FICA tax.
    b. The OASDI portion of FICA tax.
    c. Both the OASDI and Medicare portions of FICA tax.
    d. Discrimination in FICA taxation.

Medicare tax

Medicare is taxed at 1.45% of wages, and, unlike the retirement and disability portions of FICA tax, there is no wage base limit. Employers are also required to match this contribution, bringing the total funding to 2.9% of all wages earned.

Employer reporting and responsibilities

The 15.3% FICA tax is broken down as follows:

- Social Security (employee pays 6.2%)
- Social Security (employer pays 6.2%)
- Medicare (employee pays 1.45%)
- Medicare (employer pays 1.45%)

Factoring the FICA tax

The employer's portion of FICA tax is the same amount required to be withheld from employee wages. Different rules apply for employees who receive tips.

In other words, a company withholds 6.2% Social Security tax from employee wages and pays an additional 6.2% as the employer share of the tax (6.2 employee portion + 6.2 employer portion = 12.4% total). Additionally, the employer must withhold a 1.45% Medicare tax from employee wages and pay an additional 1.45% as the employer portion (1.45 employee portion + 1.45 employer portion = 2.9% total).

> ### Example 1-1
>
> In 2019, Beauteous Boots, Inc. has one employee, Sam Stockwell, to whom it pays gross wages of $1,000 every two weeks. Beauteous Boots will be required to withhold from each of Sam's paychecks $62 in Social Security taxes ($1,000 × 6.2%) and $14.50 in Medicare taxes ($1,000 × 1.45%).

Beauteous Boots, Inc. will also owe equal amounts ($62 in Social Security and $14.50 in Medicare) as the employer's portion of those taxes. In other words, each $1,000 wage payment will create a combined FICA tax liability of $153.

Because the total wages that Beauteous Boots, Inc., pays Sam for the calendar year do not exceed $200,000, it does not have to withhold the 0.9% Medicare surtax from Sam's wages.

Medicare tax on earned income

As of 2013, and ostensibly for the foreseeable future, high-income households will pay more into Medicare as a result of the health care reform law, known as the Patient Protection and Affordable Care Act (ACA) or, more colloquially, "Obamacare."

The Medicare payroll tax, which, unlike the retirement portion of FICA tax, applies to unlimited amounts of earned income, has increased for individuals making more than $200,000 in wages, and joint filers making more than $250,000.

The current 2.9% Medicare tax on wages is payable one-half by the employer and one-half by the employee. The ACA does not change the employer portion. Instead, the new 0.9% Medicare tax will be payable solely by the employee and is levied in addition to the current Medicare payroll tax.

Under the new law, which became effective in 2013, high-income individuals pay another 0.9 percentage point, so their share will total 2.35% of their wages.

Note that the tax applies to earned income more than the income thresholds, rather than to adjusted gross income (AGI).

Example 1-2

As of November 30, 2019, Pam Peterson received $170,000 in wages from Acme Associates, Inc. On December 1, 2019, Acme paid Pam a $50,000 bonus. Prior to December 1, Acme was not required to withhold the Medicare tax surcharge. On December 1, Acme is required to withhold additional Medicare Tax on $20,000 of the $50,000 bonus. However, Acme may not withhold additional Medicare Tax on the other $30,000. It must also withhold the additional 0.9% Medicare tax on any other wages paid to Pam in December 2019.

In this example, the employer must begin withholding the surtax in the pay period in which it pays wages in excess of the $200,000 (assuming single filing status) "floor" to Pam and it must continue to withhold it each pay period until the end of the calendar year.

Keep in mind that the following thresholds of wages (and not AGI) trigger the tax:

Filing status	Threshold amount
Married filing jointly—combined income	$250,000
Married filing separately	$125,000
Single, head of household, qualifying widow or widower	$200,000

The 0.9% Medicare surtax applies to wages, compensation, and self-employment earnings greater than a threshold amount that is based on the employee's filing status. Once the threshold is reached, the tax

applies to all wages that are currently subject to Medicare tax, the Railroad Retirement Tax Act, or the Self-Employment Compensation Act.

An employer must withhold Additional Medicare Tax from wages it pays to an individual in excess of $200,000 in a calendar year, without regard to the individual's filing status or wages paid by another employer. An individual may owe more than the amount withheld by the employer, depending on the individual's filing status, wages, compensation, and self-employment income. In that case, the individual should make estimated tax payments and request additional income tax withholding using Form W-4, *Employee's Withholding Allowance Certificate*.

The value of taxable wages not paid in cash, such as noncash fringe benefits, are subject to Additional Medicare Tax, if, in combination with other wages, they exceed the individual's applicable threshold.

It is interesting to note that this rule applies even if both spouses work for the same company.

Example 1-3

Arthur Carson, an employee of Fantastic Fabrications, Inc., earns $220,000 during 2019. He is married to Alice Carson, but she is a full-time homemaker and mother with no earned income. Fantastic Fabrications, Inc. must start withholding the additional 0.9% Medicare tax when Arthur's earnings exceed $200,000. Arthur's income will be over-withheld because the couple's combined income is beneath the married, filing jointly threshold of $250,000.

Employers only know their own payrolls

As a practical matter, in most real-life situations, the employer would have little, if any, opportunity to learn the earned income of the employer's spouse or that provided by an unrelated employer.

Example 1-4

Employee Lois Palmer earns $130,000 during 2019. In the same year, Lois' husband Edward earns $100,000 from one employer in his day job and $60,000 from another employer performing his night job. The Palmers' combined earnings are $290,000, clearly $40,000 more than the married, filing jointly threshold. However, none of their employers are required to withhold the 0.9% surtax because neither Lois nor Edward earned more than $200,000 from any one employer.

Taxpayer-employees having concerns about being under-withheld for the Medicare surtax can make estimated payments or they can request additional income tax withholding on Form W-4. The employee can then apply the additional income tax withheld against the Medicare surtax liability on Form 1040.

Employees earning tips

The employer is responsible for taxes on reported tips, and for paying the employer's portion of FICA and Federal Unemployment Tax Act taxes on them. This can be challenging because the employer has no control over the amount of tips their employees receive.

The employer must also withhold for the 0.9% FICA Medicare surtax. Tips are subject to FICA Medicare surtax withholding if, in combination with other wages paid by the employer, they exceed the $200,000 withholding threshold.

However, any employer's obligation to withhold the employee's portion of FICA (and income taxes) is limited to the amount of employee funds under that employer's control. That describes the nontip wages that the employer would otherwise pay to the employee.

If insufficient funds are available, they should be applied to the taxes in the following order:

- First, to the employee's portion of the FICA tax due on the nontip wage payments
- Next, to the employer's portion of the FICA tax due on the nontip wage payments
- Next, to the employee's portion of the FICA tax due on the tip income
- Last, to the employer's portion of the FICA tax due on the tip income

Tips represent payments that customers make without being obligated to do so. Customers should have the unrestricted right to determine the amount of their tips. If the amount is dictated by the employer's policy, the tips may be classified as service charges.

An employee's cash tips are not treated as taxable wages unless they amount to $20 or more in a calendar month, and the employee reports them to the employer by the 10th of the month following the month in which they were received. Once the $20 threshold has been reached, all cash tips are subject to FICA tax, including the initial $20.

No above-the-line deduction for self-employed

Further, because self-employed individuals may currently deduct one-half of the self-employment tax imposed on them, unfortunately, those self-employed individuals will not be permitted to deduct any portion of this 0.9% additional Medicare tax.

Medicare tax on net investment income

Since January 1, 2013, the Healthcare and Education Reconciliation Act of 2010 that clarified the ACA applied a 3.8% Medicare tax to unearned income for certain high-income individuals. Specifically, the 3.8% tax applies to the lesser of (1) an individual's "net investment income" and (2) the excess of the individual's modified AGI more than $200,000 ($250,000 applicable to a joint return).

Knowledge check

3. Which would be considered in determining the amount of unearned income to which the 3.8% tax on unearned income applies?

   a. IRA distributions.
   b. Form 1099 income from part-time employment.
   c. Long-term capital gain.
   d. Gains on home sales not exceeding $250,000 or $500,000 (on a joint return).

What is net investment income?

In general, investment income includes, but is not limited to, interest, dividends, capital gains (regardless of how long the asset had been held), rental and royalty income, nonqualified annuities, income from businesses involved in trading of financial instruments or commodities, and businesses that are passive activities to the taxpayer (within the meaning of IRC Section 469). To calculate a taxpayer's net investment income, the investment income is reduced by certain expenses that would be properly allocable to the income.

To the extent that gains are not otherwise offset by capital losses, the following (net) gains are common examples of items taken into account in computing net investment income:

- Gains from the sale of stocks, bonds, and mutual funds
- Capital gain distributions from mutual funds
- Gains from the sale of investment real estate (including gain from the sale of a second home that is not a primary residence)
- Gains from the sale of interests in partnerships and S corporations (to the extent of passive ownership)

What is not considered investment income?

The following sources of income are not classified as investment income:

- Wages
- Unemployment compensation
- Operating income from a nonpassive business

- Social Security benefits
- Alimony
- Tax-exempt interest
- Self-employment income
- Alaska permanent fund dividends
- Distributions from certain qualified plans

What about gains from the sale of a primary residence?

As we might expect, to the extent that gains on home sales are excluded under IRC Section 121, such gains are not classified as net investment income. However, any gain that does not qualify for the exclusion or to the extent it exceeds the exclusion amount (generally $500,000 for joint filers and $250,000 for those using single filing status) such gains would be subject to the tax. The following examples show how.

Example 1-5

Alan Archer, a single filer, earns $210,000 in wages and sells his principal residence, which he has owned and resided in for the last 10 years, for $420,000. Alan's cost basis in the home is $200,000. Alan's realized gain on the sale is $220,000. Fortunately, under IRC Section 121, Alan may exclude up to $250,000 of gain on the sale. Because this gain is excluded for regular income tax purposes, it is also excluded for purposes of determining net investment income. In this example, the net investment income tax (NIIT) does not apply to the gain from the sale of Alan's home.

Example 1-6

Bonnie and Clyde Parker, a married couple filing jointly, sell their principal residence, which they have owned and resided in for the last 10 years, for $1.3 million. Bonnie and Clyde's cost basis in the home is $700,000. Bonnie and Clyde's realized gain on the sale is $600,000. The recognized gain subject to regular income taxes is $100,000 ($600,000 realized gain less the $500,000 IRC Section 121 exclusion).

Bonnie and Clyde have $125,000 of other net investment income, which brings their total net investment income to $225,000. The Parkers' modified adjusted gross income is $300,000 and exceeds the threshold amount of $250,000 by $50,000.

Bonnie and Clyde are subject to NIIT on the lesser of $225,000 (total net investment income) or $50,000 (the amount by which Bonnie and Clyde's modified adjusted gross income exceeds the $250,000 married filing jointly threshold). Therefore, the Parkers owe NIIT of $1,900 ($50,000 × 3.8%).

Example 1-7

Daniel Dawkins, a single filer, earns $45,000 in wages and sells his principal residence, which he has owned and resided in for the last 10 years, for $1 million. Daniel's cost basis in the home is $600,000. Dan's realized gain on the sale is $400,000. The recognized gain subject to regular income taxes is $150,000 ($400,000 realized gain less the $250,000 IRC Section 121 exclusion), which is also net investment income. Daniel's modified adjusted gross income is $195,000. Because Dan's modified adjusted gross income is less than the threshold amount of $200,000, he does not owe any NIIT.

When AGI is entirely investment income

When the taxpayer's income is entirely classified as net investment income, it is still possible that not all of it will be subject to the tax, as the following example illustrates:

Example 1-8

Edith Shilton, a single filer, inherited a fortune from her uncle, the founder of a successful hotel chain, and, therefore, did not work. Edith earned only investment income from a substantial stock and bond portfolio. In 2019, the portfolio (none of which would be considered qualified retirement assets for federal income tax purposes) produces $2 million in net investment income. This amount also represents Edith's modified adjusted income for that tax year. The amount of Medicare contribution tax to which Edith would be liable is calculated by multiplying 3.8% to the lesser of

1. the net investment income of $2 million, or
2. the $2 million reduced by the $200,000 threshold amount for a single taxpayer.

Therefore, Edith will incur a Medicare contribution tax of $68,400, which is calculated by applying the 3.8% tax to $1,800,000 ($2 million in net unearned income reduced by the $200,000 single taxpayer threshold).

Not everyone is covered under Social Security

When the Social Security program began, certain groups of workers were already covered under other retirement plans. Railroad workers were covered under the Railroad Retirement Board. Workers covered under the Railroad Retirement program do not fund or receive retirement benefits from Social Security, but they may buy into Medicare. Federal government employees (including members of Congress) were covered by the Civil Service Retirement System. Those who have been continuously employed by the federal government starting before 1984 do not fund or receive retirement benefits from Social Security. Today, members of Congress pay into the system.

Employees whose services are not covered for Social Security, but who are required to pay the Medicare-only portion of FICA, are referred to as Medicare Qualified Government Employees.

The clergy and Social Security

Before 1968, a member of the clergy had to participate in Social Security. Today, most ordained, commissioned, or licensed ministers, rabbis, and other members of religious orders still pay FICA taxes for Social Security and Medicare coverage (often under self-employment tax provisions) for the services performed in a religious capacity unless that individual requested and received a tax exemption from self-employment tax. This is true whether the clergyperson is an employee of a religious organization or a self-employed person under the common law rules.

However, since 1951, an ordained member of the clergy (including members of religious orders) may object to participating in Social Security benefits based upon conscientious or religious grounds. To object, the clergyperson must file Form 4361. The individual must disclose his or her specific grounds for opting out. This election applies only to the income received in conjunction with vocational ministry. The minister may opt out relative to ministry salary and extra self-employment income earned through pastoral duties, such as honorariums for weddings and funerals. Before 1968, a member of the clergy had to elect to be covered by Social Security.

The form must be filed before the due date of the individual's personal tax return for the second taxable year in which the individual earned $400 or more from work as a member of the clergy. The election is irrevocable. The ordained clergyperson can be treated as self-employed for FICA but may be considered an employee for other tax purposes.

Self-employment tax does not apply to any postretirement benefits or the rental value of any parsonage or parsonage allowance granted to the clergyperson. The clergyperson who opts out will not be entitled to Social Security or Medicare benefits based on ministerial income.

Parents employing children

Parents employing children under age 18 working for them in unincorporated businesses are not required to withhold or match FICA tax.

For example, Natalie Sanchez owns a small public relations firm. She is a Schedule C taxpayer. She employs her son, Nathan, $10 per hour to input data into her computer, file, and help maintain an orderly office. In 2019, she pays Nathan $4,800. Natalie is not required to withhold FICA tax on Nathan's wages.

Other exceptions

Members of Native American tribal councils and students employed by the colleges they are attending are not required to pay FICA taxes on their earned income. Members of the armed services do participate in Social Security through FICA tax in the same manner as most other workers.

Summary

Our Social Security system provides retirement, disability, and survivor benefits to tens of millions of Americans. Most benefits are funded through FICA taxes, shared by workers and their employers, although newer Medicare taxes apply to workers alone. With few exceptions, earned income such as wages, tips, commissions, and more are subject to FICA tax. FICA tax itself falls into two categories—the OASDI (generally, retirement) portion and the Medicare portion. FICA tax on the OASDI portion applies only on wages up to an annually indexed taxable wage base. In contrast, the Medicare portion of FICA tax generally applies to all income.

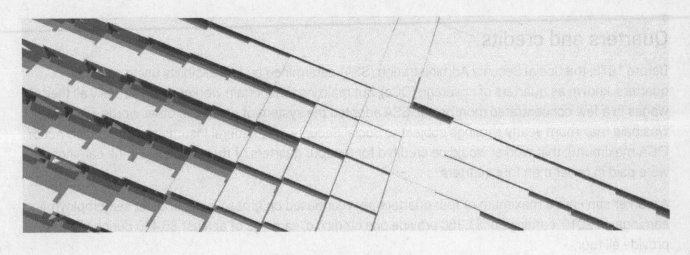

Chapter 2

Benefit Eligibility

Learning objectives

- Recognize how quarters of coverage (QCs) or Social Security credits determine a worker's insured status for Social Security benefits.

- Recall what constitutes a quarter of coverage or a Social Security credit.

- Determine whether a worker is currently insured, fully insured, or permanently insured.

- Recognize when a worker is ineligible for benefits.

Overview

A worker must be insured under the Social Security system before retirement, survivors, or disability benefits can be paid to that worker or the worker's family. All benefits—Social Security retirement, survivors, or disability—have a work requirement that varies with the specific program. A worker is insured when he or she has completed enough FICA-covered work for a given benefit. The amount of work needed is measured by credits, also called quarters of coverage.

Quarters and credits

Before 1978, the Social Security Administration (SSA) determined benefit eligibility using calendar quarters, known as quarters of coverage (QCs), but realizing that certain workers earn virtually all their wages in a few concentrated months, the SSA adopted the system of *credits*. In other words, if a worker was paid maximum yearly earnings subject to Social Security, (the Federal Insurance Contribution Act or FICA maximum), that worker would be credited for the four quarters of that year, even if the earnings were paid in fewer than four quarters.

A worker can earn a maximum of four quarters per year based on gross wages and net self-employment earnings. In 2019, earnings of $1,360 provide one credit; so, earnings of at least $5,440 during the year provide all four.

Example 2-1

Presume that Hal is paid $2,720 in 2019, when the Social Security credit amount is $1,360 (as shown in the preceding paragraph). Hal is credited with two credits or QCs because his earnings are at least two multiples of $1,360, but fewer than three multiples. That same year, his brother Cal earned $6,000, which was subject to FICA tax. Cal is credited with four QCs because his FICA earnings are at least four multiples of $1,360.

The examples illustrate that it does not matter when the wages were earned. The QC or credit is attributable to the quarter in which the wages were paid to the worker. However, if the covered worker was paid maximum yearly earnings subject to Social Security—the FICA maximum—the worker is credited for the four quarters of that year, even if the earnings were paid in less than four quarters.

Becoming permanently insured for retirement benefits

To be eligible to receive the full menu of Social Security retirement benefits (other than disability insurance), an individual needs 40 credits. Becoming insured for retirement can take more than 10 years for a worker with low annual wages. Workers with less than 40 quarters are not eligible for retirement benefits. Once insured status is established, the number of credits has no impact on the amount of the monthly retirement benefit the individual will receive. The individual benefit is computed on actual earnings and is covered in another chapter.

Knowledge check

1. What does a worker generally need to be eligible to receive the full menu of Social Security retirement benefits (other than disability insurance)?

    a. Six credits.
    b. Thirteen credits.
    c. Forty credits.
    d. One hundred-eighty credits.

Special pre-1978 rules

In years before 1978, a worker would receive a QC for each calendar quarter during which he or she was paid at least $50.

There is a special rule that applies to farm workers for years before 1978. Instead of the $50-per-quarter rule, a farm worker received a QC for each $100 in cash wages paid during a year, without regard to the quarter in which the wages were paid. QCs were assigned beginning with the last calendar quarter and then counting backward.

Eligibility

Rules for determining insured statuses are different for self-employed workers than they are for employees. In all later years, a self-employed individual accumulates credits or QCs based on the amount of total yearly earnings in the same manner as an employee does. However, the self-employed individual must at least a minimum of $400 in net earnings from self-employment to receive any credits or QCs.

Both self-employed and working for another

If a person is both self-employed and an employee, that worker must add total earnings as an employee, and net earnings from self-employment to determine how many credits or QCs will be available.

Reporting earnings subject to FICA

Wages are reported to the SSA using Form W-2. For employees, the employer reports Social Security wages in box 3 of Form W-2. The Social Security tax paid by the employee is reported in box 4. Employers are required to file Form W-2 with the SSA using form W-3 no later than January 31 for the previous calendar year's earnings.

Self-employment earnings (business owner, independent contractor, freelancer, and the like) are reported on Schedule C. Self-employed farmers use Schedule F to report their business earnings.

Only the net earnings reported on Schedules C or F are considered earnings by the SSA.

The Social Security tax due is calculated using Schedule SE for filers of Schedule C or F. Some self-employed people need extra time to gather all the information necessary to file an accurate tax return. If business owner clients file unusually late, for the purpose of obtaining Social Security credits, it is important to file a tax return before the three-year time limit expires (as explained in the following section).

Knowledge check

2. Which form is used to report an employee's Social Security earnings to the Social Security Administration?

    a. K-1.
    b. 1099-SSC.
    c. W-2.
    d. 1099-Misc.

Time limit for reporting earnings

The reporting of Social Security earnings must be done in a timely fashion to allow the accumulating of credits towards future Social Security benefits. The time period is three years, three months, and 15 days following the end of the calendar year in which the employee or self-employed individual earns the income. If earnings are not reported within this period, Social Security credits are not accumulated for the unreported income.

Verifying the credits

The SSA no longer mails out a Social Security Statement automatically every year. However, one can obtain a personal Social Security Statement online by using the "*my* Social Security" feature available at SSA.gov. *my* Social Security began in May of 2012 and in June of 2017 a second method of verification became required to access your account in the interest of cybersecurity. The easiest and most convenient way for most people to get instant benefit verification is by creating an account at www.socialsecurity.gov/myaccount. The online statement offers secure access to earnings records. It also shows estimates for retirement, disability, and survivors' benefits. Covered workers and their advisers should check this statement to ensure that the individual's wages and net self-employment earnings are reported accurately. Beginning in 2014, the SSA began sending paper statements every five years to individuals who are age 25, 30, 35, 40, 45, 50, 55, and 60. An annual statement will be mailed to individuals for each year after age 60. The paper statements will be sent to those individuals who have not established a "*my* Social Security" account.

Insured statuses

"Fully insured" status is required for most benefits. "Currently insured" status is required for young widows or widowers and surviving children. A special "disability-insured" status is required for disability insurance benefits.

Dependents and survivors are eligible based on their relationship to an insured worker. They are not subject to a work requirement. However, the worker on whose account their benefits are based must have satisfied a specific insured status requirement.

Fully insured status

To be fully insured, a worker turning age 21 after 1950 generally needs at least one QC for each calendar year after attaining age 21 and the earliest of

1. the year before attaining age 62,
2. the year before death, or
3. the year before becoming disabled.

An exception is available for workers born before 1930. Their requirement is at least one QC for each year after 1950. Other exceptions may apply.

The minimum number of credits or QCs needed is six. All (or part) of a year that was included in a period of disability is not included in determining the number of QCs needed.

Permanently insured

A worker is permanently insured after accumulating 40 QCs. If the worker is fully insured, he or she will not lose fully insured status when he or she stops working under FICA-covered employment.

Example 2-2

Ann Robinson was born in 1949 and worked under FICA-covered employment from 1971 through 1977, earning 28 credits or QCs. Ann turned age 21 in 1970. Given her age, she became fully insured after earning six QCs. Ann would continue to be fully insured even if she died or became disabled before the end of 1999. However, after 1999, Ann was no longer fully insured. Why? Because Ann earned only 28 credits or QCs. After 1978, she needed 40 QCs, and so never attained "permanently insured" status.

Credits required to be fully insured

The age and number of credits required for deemed fully insured status is provided in the following chart.

If one was the following age on January 1, 1984, . . .	. . . then the following number of credits is required:
60 or over	6
59 or over, but less than 60	8
58 or over, but less than 59	12
57 or over, but less than 58	16
55 or over, but less than 57	20

Note: Credits earned before January 1, 1984 may not be used for deemed fully insured status. They may be used in addition to credits earned after 1983 to establish regular fully insured status.

Disability-insured status

A FICA-covered worker has obtained disability-insured status if he or she

- earned at least 20 QCs during the last 10 years, and
- has attained fully insured status.

Exceptions apply for those younger than age 31 and in certain other cases.

Workers who have not yet turned 31 will be fully insured if they have credits in at least one-half of the calendar quarters during the period beginning with the quarter after the quarter they turned 21 and ending with the quarter during which they became disabled.

The credits must be earned in this period. If the number of elapsing calendar quarters is an odd number, the next lower even number is used.

Currently insured status

Currently insured status requires fewer QCs than fully insured status. The currently insured worker is eligible for a smaller menu of benefits than a fully insured worker. Benefits available to a worker who is currently insured include

- Surviving child's benefits, mother's/father's (young widow's or widower's benefits), lump-sum death benefit, and
- Medicare for end-stage renal disease (kidney failure) patients.

To be currently insured, a worker must accumulate at least six QCs within the 13 calendar quarter periods ending with the calendar quarter of death.

The calendar quarters are

- first quarter—January, February, March;
- second quarter—April, May, June;
- third quarter—July, August, September; and
- fourth quarter—October, November, December.

To determine this period, take the quarter and year of death, then go back three years from that year. The period begins with the quarter of that year (three years earlier) that corresponds to the quarter of death.

Example 2-3

Barbara Brooks died on May 15, 2019—the second quarter of 2019. Subtracting three years from 2019 is 2016. Therefore, the 13-quarter period for Barbara began with the second quarter of 2016 and ended with the second quarter of 2019. If Barbara earned six credits or QCs during that period, which included the beginning and ending quarters, she would be considered as currently insured.

What the benefits do

When Social Security was enacted in the 1930s, it was not the intention that older Americans rely entirely on Social Security benefits for retirement income. The program has long been regarded as one "leg" of a "three-legged stool" of retirement security that includes the following:

1. Personal savings
2. Distributions from retirement plans such as pensions, IRAs, and other qualified plans
3. Social Security benefits

However, that is not always the case. Today, Social Security alone provides the majority of income for nearly two-thirds of older Americans who receive its benefits. Savings and pensions have been inadequate. As a result, and in light of microscopic interest rates on personal savings, many Americans—particularly low-and middle-income earners—are facing an economically challenging retirement.

Knowledge check

3. A worker younger than age 31 needs how many quarters of coverage to be eligible for full Social Security disability benefits?

    a. 100% of worked quarters to age of disability.
    b. 75% of worked quarters.
    c. 50% of worked quarters from age 21 to age of disability before age 31.
    d. 20% of worked quarters from age 21 to age of disability before age 31.

Summary

We discussed how Social Security credits or QCs determine a worker's eligibility for specific Social Security benefits. We learned that credits, or QCs, are based on a specific dollar amount of FICA-covered earnings. A worker is permanently insured after 40 credits or QCs even if he or she stops working after obtaining the 40 quarters. Although fully insured workers are eligible for Social Security retirement (old age) benefits, currently insured workers are not. Special rules determine eligibility for Social Security disability insurance benefits.

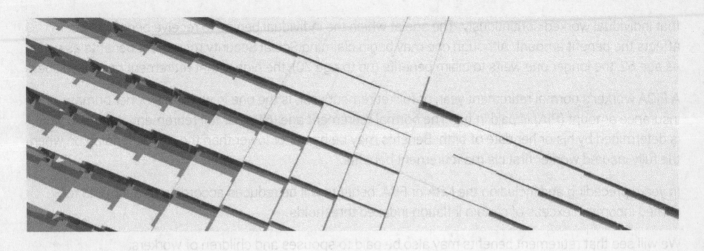

Chapter 3

Social Security Retirement Benefits

Learning objectives

- Recall the relationship between years of FICA earnings and average indexed monthly earnings (AIME).

- Recognize the importance of a fully insured worker's full or normal retirement age in determining benefits.

- Identify the manner in which AIME and the PIA determine retirement benefits.

- Determine how claiming benefits while younger than normal retirement age will result in a reduction of benefits.

- Recall how first claiming benefits when older than normal retirement age results in an increase in benefits.

- Identify auxiliary retirement benefits for spouses, divorced spouses, and children of fully insured workers.

Overview

A Federal Insurance Contributions Act (FICA)-covered worker's retirement benefit is based on his or her average earnings over a working career. Higher lifetime earnings result in higher benefits. As a result,, if a worker had some years of no earnings or low earnings, his or her benefit amount may be lower than had that individual worked continuously. The age at which the individual begins to receive benefits also affects the benefit amount. Although one may begin claiming Social Security retirement benefits as early as age 62, the longer one waits to claim benefits (up to age 70), the higher that retirement benefit will be.

A FICA worker's normal retirement year, or full retirement year, is the one in which his or her primary insurance amount (PIA) is paid in full. The normal retirement age (NRA) or full retirement age (FRA) year is determined by his or her date of birth. Benefits may be higher or lower than the PIA depending on when the fully insured worker first claims retirement benefits.

In years preceding and including the NRA or FRA, benefits will be reduced according to a formula for earned income in excess of certain inflation-indexed thresholds.

We will see that retirement benefits may also be paid to spouses and children of workers.

Retirement benefits

Normal or full retirement age

Full retirement age is the age at which a person may first become entitled to full or unreduced retirement benefits. No matter what your full retirement age (also called normal retirement age) is, you may start receiving benefits as early as age 62 or as late as age 70. For many years, NRA was age 65. Now, however, your date of birth governs your NRA. Beginning with people born in 1938 or later, that age gradually increases until it reaches 67 for people born after 1959.

The following table, provided by the Social Security Administration (SSA), indicates how NRA varies by year of birth for retirees.

Normal retirement age	
Year of birth	Age
1937 and prior	65
1938	65 and 2 months
1939	65 and 4 months
1940	65 and 6 months
1941	65 and 8 months
1942	65 and 10 months
1943–54	66
1955	66 and 2 months
1956	66 and 4 months
1957	66 and 6 months
1958	66 and 8 months
1959	66 and 10 months
1960 and later	67

Notes:
1. Persons born on January 1 of any year should refer to the normal retirement age for the previous year.
2. For the purpose of determining benefit reductions for early retirement, widows and widowers whose entitlement is based on having attained age 60 should add two years to the year of birth shown in the table.

For example, John Roberts was born on March 13, 1953. His NRA (using the preceding chart) will be March 2019.

The SSA has developed a simple retirement age calculator tool to help people determine their NRA. The tool is reproduced below (and can be accessed at https://www.ssa.gov/planners/retire/agereduction.html).

Full retirement and age 62 benefit by year of birth

Year of birth[1].	Full (normal) retirement age	Months between age 62 and full retirement age[2].	At age 62[3].			
			A $1000 retirement benefit would be reduced to	The retirement benefit is reduced by[4].	A $500 spouse's benefit would be reduced to	The spouse's benefit is reduced by[5].
1937 or earlier	65	36	$800	20.00%	$375	25.00%
1938	65 and 2 months	38	$791	20.83%	$370	25.83%
1939	65 and 4 months	40	$783	21.67%	$366	26.67%
1940	65 and 6 months	42	$775	22.50%	$362	27.50%
1941	65 and 8 months	44	$766	23.33%	$358	28.33%
1942	65 and 10 months	46	$758	24.17%	$354	29.17%
1943-1954	66	48	$750	25.00%	$350	30.00%
1955	66 and 2 months	50	$741	25.83%	$345	30.83%
1956	66 and 4 months	52	$733	26.67%	$341	31.67%
1957	66 and 6 months	54	$725	27.50%	$337	32.50%
1958	66 and 8 months	56	$716	28.33%	$333	33.33%
1959	66 and 10 months	58	$708	29.17%	$329	34.17%
1960 and later	67	60	$700	30.00%	$325	35.00%

[1.] If you were born on January 1st, you should refer to the previous year.

[2.] If you were born on the 1st of the month, we figure your benefit (and your full retirement age) as if your birthday was in the previous month. If you were born on January 1st, we figure your benefit (and your full retirement age) as if your birthday was in December of the previous year.

[3.] You must be at least 62 for the entire month to receive benefits.

[4.] Percentages are approximate due to rounding.

[5.] The maximum benefit for the spouse is 50 percent of the benefit the worker would receive at full retirement age. The percent reduction for the spouse should be applied after the automatic 50 percent reduction. Percentages are approximate due to rounding.

AIME

The Social Security retirement benefit calculation factors how long an applicant worked and the amount of FICA-taxed earnings each year. These variables are used to calculate a fully insured worker's AIME. The calculation is made in a series of steps, as follows:

Step 1: List FICA-taxed earnings each year

A worker's earnings history is reported on his or Social Security statement, which is now obtainable from the SSA online at www.socialsecurity.gov/myaccount/.

Step 2: Adjust each year of earnings for inflation

The SSA uses a process called wage indexing to determine how to adjust a fully insured worker's current and previous earnings for inflation. There are two steps in the wage indexing process.

- First, each year the SSA publishes the national average wages for the year. The list is available at the National Average Wage Index page https://www.ssa.gov/oact/COLA/AWI.html.
- Second, the worker's wages are indexed to the average wages for the year he or she turns 60. For each year, one would take the average wages of the indexing year (which is the year in which the covered worker turns age 60) divided by average wages for the year being indexed, and multiply the included earnings by this number.

Example 3-1

Lance Lerner was born in 1950; he had 1984 FICA-taxed earnings of $25,000. The average 1984 earnings were $16,135. The figure $41,674 represents the average earnings for the year when Lance turned 60—in this case, 2010. Divide $41,674 by the 1984 average earnings of $16,135, to get the index factor. Finally, multiply Lance's 1984 wages of $25,000 by this index factor to get $64,571.

Before age 60, it is only an estimate

Considering the application of the wage indexing formula, the calculation to determine the PIA is an estimate for a fully covered worker who is not yet 62 years old. The average wages for the year in which the worker attains age 60 is unknown, so an exact calculation is not possible. Nevertheless, one could impute an assumed inflation rate to average wages to estimate the average wages going forward.

A statement from the SSA showing estimated benefits at age 62, full retirement age, and age 70, includes earnings your current salary through age 60. Large changes in earnings from the date you are looking at the report to age 60 can make a significant difference in your future estimated benefit.

Step 3: Use the highest 35 years of indexed earnings to calculate a monthly average

To determine a worker's average monthly earnings, the Social Security benefits calculation factors the highest 35 years of a FICA-covered worker's earnings. Presuming that a worker does not have 35 years of FICA-covered earnings, a zero will be used in the calculation, which will lower the average. One would then total the highest 35 years of indexed earnings and divide this total by 420 (representing the number of months in a 35-year work history). This produces a worker's AIME.

Calculating the PIA

The PIA is the benefit (before rounding down to the next lower whole dollar) that a covered individual would receive if he or she elects to begin receiving retirement benefits at his or her normal (full) retirement age. At this age, the benefit is neither reduced for early retirement nor increased for delayed retirement.

The formula for the PIA is the basic benefit formula. The dollar amounts in the formula are sometimes called "bend points" because a formula, when graphed, appears as a series of line segments joined at these amounts (https://www.ssa.gov/OACT/COLA/bendpoints.html).

Exhibit 3-1

Benefit formula bend points

Automatic Determinations	The formula for the Primary Insurance Amount (PIA) is the basic benefit formula. The dollar amounts in the formula are sometimes called "bend points" because a formula, when graphed, appears as a series of line segments joined at these amounts.	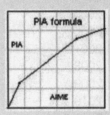
PIA benefit formula		
Maximum family benefit formula		

Dollar amounts in Primary Insurance Amount and maximum family benefit formulas

Year[a]	Dollar amounts in PIA formula		Dollar amounts in maximum family benefit formula		
	First	Second	First	Second	Third
1979	$180	$1,085	$230	$332	$433
1980	194	1,171	248	358	467
1981	211	1,274	270	390	508
1982	230	1,388	294	425	554
1983	254	1,528	324	468	610
1984	267	1,612	342	493	643
1985	280	1,691	358	517	675
1986	297	1,790	379	548	714
1987	310	1,866	396	571	745
1988	319	1,922	407	588	767
1989	339	2,044	433	626	816
1990	356	2,145	455	656	856
1991	370	2,230	473	682	890
1992	387	2,333	495	714	931
1993	401	2,420	513	740	966

Exhibit 3-1 (continued)

Year[a]	Dollar amounts in PIA formula		Dollar amounts in maximum family benefit formula		
	First	Second	First	Second	Third
1994	422	2,545	539	779	1,016
1995	426	2,567	544	785	1,024
1996	437	2,635	559	806	1,052
1997	455	2,741	581	839	1,094
1998	477	2,875	609	880	1,147
1999	505	3,043	645	931	1,214
2000	531	3,202	679	980	1,278
2001	561	3,381	717	1,034	1,349
2002	592	3,567	756	1,092	1,424
2003	606	3,653	774	1,118	1,458
2004	612	3,689	782	1,129	1,472
2005	627	3,779	801	1,156	1,508
2006	656	3,955	838	1,210	1,578
2007	680	4,100	869	1,255	1,636
2008	711	4,288	909	1,312	1,711
2009	744	4,483	950	1,372	1,789
2010	761	4,586	972	1,403	1,830
2011	749	4,517	957	1,382	1,803
2012	767	4,624	980	1,415	1,845
2013	791	4,768	1,011	1,459	1,903
2014	816	4,917	1,042	1,505	1,962
2015	826	4,980	1,056	1,524	1,987
2016	856	5,157	1,093	1,578	2,058
2017	885	5,336	1,131	1,633	2,130
2018	895	5,397	1,144	1,651	2,154
2019	926	5,583	1,184	1,708	2,228

[a] Year of eligibility; that is, the year in which a worker attains age 62, becomes disabled before age 62, or dies before attaining age 62.

Source: Social Security Administration (https://www.ssa.gov/oact/cola/bendpoints.html).

Formula

The PIA for a fully-insured worker who first becomes eligible for Social Security retirement benefits or disability insurance benefits in 2019, or who dies in 2019 before becoming eligible for benefits, will be the sum of

- 90% of the first $926 of the worker's AIME, plus
- 32% of the worker's AIME greater than $926 and through $5,583, plus
- 15% of the worker's AIME greater than $5,583.

The amount is then rounded down to the next lower multiple of $0.10 if it is not already a multiple of $0.10.

Example 3-2

Cheryl Burton had maximum-taxable earnings in each year since age 22. She retires at age 62 in 2019. Cheryl would have an AIME equal to $9,431. Based on this AIME amount and the bend points $926 and $5,583, her PIA would equal $2901. If she retires before her full or normal retirement age, Cheryl would receive a reduced benefit based on the $2,901 PIA. The cost of living increase that Cheryl could receive would be effective December 2019.

Cost of living increases

Cost of living increases, or COLAs, are intended to keep benefits in pace with inflation so that a benefit recipient's buying power holds roughly steady. Congress enacted the COLA provisions in 1972 as part of the Social Security Amendments with automatic COLA adjustments becoming effective in 1975. According to the SSA, COLAs received in 1975–2019 are as follows.

Automatic cost-of-living adjustments	
July 1975—8.0%	January 1996—2.6%
July 1976—6.4%	January 1997—2.9%
July 1977—5.9%	January 1998—2.1%
July 1978—6.5%	January 1999—1.3%
July 1979—9.9%	January 2000—2.5%[1]
July 1980—14.3%	January 2001—3.5%
July 1981—11.2%	January 2002—2.6%
July 1982—7.4%	January 2003—1.4%
January 1984—3.5%	January 2004—2.1%
January 1985—3.5%	January 2005—2.7%
January 1986—3.1%	January 2006—4.1%
January 1987—1.3%	January 2007—3.3%
January 1988—4.2%	January 2008—2.3%
January 1989—4.0%	January 2009—5.8%
January 1990—4.7%	January 2010—0.0%
January 1991—5.4%	January 2011—0.0%
January 1992—3.7%	January 2012—3.6%
January 1993—3.0%	January 2013—1.7%
January 1994—2.6%	January 2014—1.5%
January 1995—2.8%	January 2015—1.7%
	January 2016—0.0%
	January 2017—0.3%
	January 2018—2.0%
	January 2019 – 2.8%

[1] The COLA for December 1999 was originally determined as 2.4% based on Consumer Price Indexes (CPIs) published by the Bureau of Labor Statistics. Pursuant to Public Law 106-554, however, this COLA is effectively now 2.5%.

The benefit increase of 2.8% for 2019 will affect more than 67 million Social Security recipients and 8 million Supplemental Social Income (SSI) beneficiaries in 2019, many of whom live on fixed incomes. The amount of the increase each year is not announced until after October of the prior year when the key inflation statistic that sets the COLA, the CPI, for the July–September quarter is released. To calculate the amount of the COLA, the government will compare that inflation figure with the figure for that same calendar quarter in the year immediately prior.

Historically, Social Security payments have been adjusted each year to reflect inflation as measured by the Consumer Price Index for Urban Wage Earners and Clerical Workers. Previous inflation adjustments have ranged from 0% in 2010, 2011, and 2016 to 14.3% in 1980.

Deciding when to begin benefits

Generally, early or late retirement will produce approximately the same total Social Security benefits over the recipient's lifetime. If one claims Social Security retirement benefits early, the monthly benefit amounts will be smaller to take into account the longer period over which they will be distributed. If a fully insured worker claims benefits later, he or she will receive benefits for a shorter period of time, but the monthly amounts will be larger to make up for the months when no benefits were paid.

Each potential benefit recipient's situation is different. Therefore, the following should be kept in mind:

- It is critical to consider cash flow before deciding when to claim Social Security retirement benefits.
- Claiming retirement benefits prior to full retirement age would result in lower monthly benefit payments.
- Delaying benefits until after full retirement age generally results in delayed retirement credits that would increase the monthly retirement benefit.
- For individuals in poor health, or those whose family histories point to an abbreviated lifespan, there is a stronger case for claiming Social Security retirement benefits at an early age.
- Is it likely that the benefit recipient will have earned income in amounts that cause a reduction in Social Security retirement benefits?
- Is there concern that Congress will reduce benefit amounts in the future?
- It is important to contact Social Security to communicate about when benefits would be claimed.

Social Security income planner

If, in your practice as a CPA or CPA financial planner, you wish to perform more sophisticated analysis as to when and how you or your clients should claim Social Security retirement benefits, you may wish to consider investing in software that will help you calculate how and when to claim Social Security retirement benefits, and will help you craft a strategy that will help your clients get the most value out of the Social Security program.

Reduction in benefits for claiming benefits early

The earliest age a fully covered worker can begin getting Social Security retirement benefits is 62. Many Americans are forced by necessity to take benefits as soon as they become eligible. Their benefits will be permanently lowered by this decision, but cash flow needs ultimately drive the decision to claim early benefits. According to the SSA, approximately 73% of retired workers claimed their benefits earlier than full retirement age.

Benefits will be reduced from the PIA in the following ways:

- A benefit is reduced $5/9$ of 1% for each month before normal retirement age, up to 36 months.
- If the number of months exceeds 36, then the benefit is further reduced $5/12$ of 1% per month for months in excess of 36 months.

Example 3-3

Bill Meyers is age 62. Bill's NRA is age 66. His PIA entitles him to receive $1,000 in monthly benefits. If Bill begins claiming his retirement benefits start at 62 (his earliest opportunity), his monthly benefit would be reduced by 25%, to $750, where it would remain as long as he drew benefits (adjusted upwards by future COLA adjustments).

Example 3-4

Julia Davidson's NRA is age 66. She makes her first benefit claim 24 months earlier. Assuming her PIA is $1,000 per month her benefit will be reduced by $133.40, calculated by multiplying $1,000 by $1,000 × 24 × $1/180$. Julia's benefit would be permanently reduced by $133.40.

Example 3-5

Jill Jenkins' normal retirement age is 67. She claims retirement benefits at age 62, her earliest opportunity. The number of reduction months is 60 (the maximum number for retirement at 62 when normal retirement age is 67). Jill's benefit is reduced by 30%. This maximum reduction is calculated as 36 months × $5/9$ of 1% + 24 months × $5/12$ of 1%.

Online calculators to help with these determinations are available on many websites, including https://www.ssa.gov/planners/calculators

Break-even analysis

There are many reasons why most older Americans choose to take Social Security retirement benefits prior to their normal retirement age. The early benefits carry present value, and the break-even analysis often makes the argument unless the benefit recipient will lead a very long life.

Example 3-6

Donald Weill makes his first claim for Social Security retirement benefits 47 months before his NRA at age 66. You can see that he just turned 62, so benefits, albeit reduced, are available. Further, presume that Donald's PIA is $1,000 per month. Given the advance of 47 months ahead of his NRA, his benefit would be reduced to $754.20 or 75.42% of his PIA. Over the 47 months between now and Donald's full retirement age, his benefits will amount to $35,447.40. By dividing $35,447.40 by the benefit reduction of $245.80 per month produces 144.21 months. That means it would take a little over 144 months or 12 years before Donald's decision to take benefits early would be a poor trade-off. Additionally, if one factors in inflation, time value of money, COLA adjustments, and other variables, the ultimate break-even point is even later.

Effect of early or delayed retirement on retirement benefits

			Benefit, as percentage of PIA, payable at ages 62–67 and age 70						
Year of birth	Normal retirement age (NRA)	Credit for each year of delayed retirement after NRA (percent)	Benefit, as a percentage of PIA, beginning at age						
			62	63	64	65	66	67	70
1924	65	3	80	$86^2/_3$	$93^1/_3$	100	103	106	115
1925–1926	65	$3^1/_2$	80	$86^2/_3$	$93^1/_3$	100	$103^1/_2$	107	$117^1/_2$
1927–1928	65	4	80	$86^2/_3$	$93^1/_3$	100	104	108	120
1929–1930	65	$4^1/_2$	80	$86^2/_3$	$93^1/_3$	100	$104^1/_2$	109	$122^1/_2$
1931–1932	65	5	80	$86^2/_3$	$93^1/_3$	100	105	110	125
1933–1934	65	$5^1/_2$	80	$86^2/_3$	$93^1/_3$	100	$105^1/_2$	111	$127^1/_2$
1935–1936	65	6	80	$86^2/_3$	$93^1/_3$	100	106	112	130
1937	65	$6^1/_2$	80	$86^2/_3$	$93^1/_3$	100	$106^1/_2$	113	$132^1/_2$
1938	65, 2 mo.	$6^1/_2$	$79^1/_6$	$85^5/_9$	$92^2/_9$	$98^8/_9$	$105^5/_{12}$	$111^{11}/_{12}$	$131^5/_{12}$
1939	65, 4 mo.	7	$78^1/_3$	$84^4/_9$	$91^1/_9$	$97^7/_9$	$104^2/_3$	$111^2/_3$	$132^2/_3$

Effect of early or delayed retirement on retirement benefits (continued)

Year of birth	Normal retirement age (NRA)	Credit for each year of delayed retirement after NRA (percent)	Benefit, as a percentage of PIA, beginning at age						
			62	63	64	65	66	67	70
1940	65, 6 mo.	7	$77^1/_2$	$83^1/_3$	90	$96^2/_3$	$103^1/_2$	$110^1/_2$	$131^1/_2$
1941	65, 8 mo.	$7^1/_2$	$76^2/_3$	$82^2/_9$	$88^8/_9$	$95^5/_9$	$102^1/_2$	110	$132^1/_2$
1942	65, 10 mo.	$7^1/_2$	$75^5/_6$	$81^1/_9$	$87^7/_9$	$94^4/_9$	$101^1/_4$	$108^3/_4$	$131^1/_4$
1943–1954	66	8	75	80	$86^2/_3$	$93^1/_3$	100	108	132
1955	66, 2 mo.	8	$74^1/_6$	$79^1/_6$	$85^5/_9$	$92^2/_9$	$98^8/_9$	$106^2/_3$	$130^2/_3$
1956	66, 4 mo.	8	$73^1/_3$	$78^1/_3$	$84^4/_9$	$91^1/_9$	$97^7/_9$	$105^1/_3$	$129^1/_3$
1957	66, 6 mo.	8	$72^1/_2$	$77^1/_2$	$83^1/_3$	90	$96^2/_3$	104	128
1958	66, 8 mo.	8	$71^2/_3$	$76^2/_3$	$82^2/_9$	$88^8/_9$	$95^5/_9$	$102^2/_3$	$126^2/_3$
1959	66, 10 mo.	8	$70^5/_6$	$75^5/_6$	$81^1/_9$	$87^7/_9$	$94^4/_9$	$101^1/_3$	$125^1/_3$
1960 and later	67	8	70	75	80	$86^2/_3$	$93^1/_3$	100	124

Note: Persons born on January 1 of any year should refer to the previous year of birth.
Source: SSA.

Delaying Social Security retirement benefits

Social Security benefits are increased by a certain percentage (depending on date of birth) if a fully insured worker delays retirement beyond full retirement age. The benefit increase no longer applies once the potential benefit recipient reaches age 70, even if the fully insured worker continues to delay taking benefits. When, from family history, a fully insured worker anticipates a long lifespan, delaying benefits, of course, would be more economically productive.

Increase for delayed retirement		
Year of birth*	Yearly rate of increase	Monthly rate of increase
1933–1934	5.5%	11/24 of 1%
1935–1936	6.0%	1/2 of 1%
1937–1938	6.5%	13/24 of 1%
1939–1940	7.0%	7/12 of 1%
1941–1942	7.5%	5/8 of 1%
1943 or later	8.0%	2/3 of 1%

Note: If you were born on January 1, you should refer to the rate of increase for the previous year.

Example 3-7

Ralph Krammel's full or normal retirement age is 66. At age 66, his monthly retirement benefit would be $2,533. Using figures from online calculators found on https://www.ssa.gov/planners/calculators, we can calculate that if he delays claiming benefits until age 70, Ralph's benefit increases to $3,725 per month.

If Ralph lives to age 90 (his parents died in their mid- to late-90s) and assuming an average 3% annual increase in cost of living raises, he would have been better off waiting until age 70 to start. He would have received $1,136,641 in retirement benefits during his lifetime.

Changing when to start Social Security retirement benefits

Unforeseen changes can occur in the lives of older Americans. If Helen started taking her Social Security retirement benefit at 62, her earliest opportunity, then inherited hundreds of thousands of dollars from her favorite Uncle Henry six months later, she can change her mind about taking her benefits so early. Generally, she can withdraw her Social Security claim and reapply within one year of the receipt of her first check and reapply at a later age.

However, the benefit recipient must repay all benefits received up to the point of the withdrawal including any benefits that had been paid to a spouse or children. This applies regardless of whether the individuals receiving the auxiliary benefits are living with the covered worker at the time of the benefit withdrawal.

Further, if Medicare premiums for Part B (most likely), Part C, or Part D had been withheld from prior Social Security retirement benefit checks, they must also be returned.

If an individual is entitled to Medicare benefits at age 65 but is not receiving Social Security retirement benefits at that time, it is important that he or she begin the process of applying for Medicare benefits. Failure to enroll in Medicare at age 65 generally results in an increased premium.

The benefit recipient who later chooses to withdraw her claim must also return, to the SSA, any income tax that had been withheld on the prior retirement benefits.

Keep in mind that a benefit recipient cannot withdraw the benefit claim unless the withdrawal is filed within the first 12 months of receiving the first benefit. The one-year limitation applies to any withdrawal of benefit claim after December 8, 2010.

Helen could suspend her Social Security benefits rather than withdrawing her benefits. She will earn delayed retirement credits from the time of her withdrawal to the time she begins benefits again. The delayed retirement credits will be based on the benefit Helen was receiving just prior to her suspension of benefits. Any benefits received by a spouse or qualifying children will also be suspended.

Spousal retirement benefits

Spouses are entitled to Social Security retirement benefits representing up to 50% of the higher earner's PIA if that amount is higher than the benefit based on his or her own FICA-taxed earnings. The 50% will be reduced if the spouse claims benefits before his or her full retirement age. Spousal benefits are based on the other spouse's work record adjusted for the age of the spouse requesting spousal benefits. Spousal benefits do not accrue delayed retirement credits beyond full retirement age, so spousal benefits should be claimed no later than full retirement age.

Example 3-8

Tom and Tanya Gregory are married. They will both claim benefits at their respective full retirement ages. Tom was a very successful salesperson and earned well over the taxable wage base during the majority of his working years. His PIA is $2,400 per month. Although Tanya did work, much of it was low-paying and part time. Her PIA is $775 per month. Tanya's spousal benefit representing one-half of her husband's PIA, exceeds 100% of her own PIA. Therefore, the SSA would pay Tanya a monthly benefit of $1,200.

If the spouse will receive a pension for work not covered by Social Security such as government or foreign employment, the amount of his or her Social Security benefits base on the FICA-paying spouse's earning may be reduced.

When both spouses work

When both spouses work, married couples can claim spousal and worker payments at different times. In a situation where both spouses had FICA earnings and have reached their full retirement age, they can claim a spousal payment and then switch to payments based on their own work record later. The claim for "spousal benefits only" is allowed only for people born in 1953 and earlier. Anyone born after 1953 will not be allowed to file for spousal benefits only at full retirement age but must take the higher of spousal or his or her own benefit. Only one member of the couple may claim spousal benefits while waiting for his or her own benefit to accrue delayed retirement credits to age 70. Again, this applies only to people born in 1953 and earlier.

After reaching full retirement age, a worker who is already entitled to benefits may voluntarily suspend, current or future retirement benefit payments up to age 70 beginning the month after the month when the request is made. The worker may also elect to suspend any retroactive benefits that are due.

Keep in mind, however, that if a FICA-covered worker has begun receiving benefits, then decides to suspend in favor of spousal benefits, he or she may make that change only within the first 12 months of receiving the first retirement benefit check based on his or her own FICA earnings.

Waiting and delaying benefits past normal retirement age will provide a higher benefit payment to which they can switch. This strategy is generally known as file and suspend and can be done only at full retirement age or later. (See chapter 1: File and suspend is allowed only for those age 66 or older by April 30, 2016.)

Restricted application

If the second spouse has also paid into the system and now wants only spousal benefits, he or she files a restricted application for spousal benefits only. Restricted application is now allowed only for people born in 1953 and earlier. Any person born in 1954 or later is not allowed to file a restricted application for spousal benefits only.

> ### Example 3-9
>
> Audrey Scott is a married woman planning to retire at age 70 although her full retirement age is 66. She takes great satisfaction in her work as a reading and math tutor for children with learning disabilities. She can claim a spousal payment based on her husband's earnings at age 66 and then later make a new claim based on her own earnings when she leaves her job at age 70. Due to spousal benefits, Audrey enjoys four years of spousal payments although she continues to work and accumulate the delayed retirement credits. Audrey was born in 1953.

Keep in mind that a spouse cannot elect to receive spousal benefits less than his or her normal retirement age then later switch to her own benefits. Benefits paid to a spouse will not decrease the retirement benefit of the worker on whose FICA earnings the benefits are based.

It generally makes sense to delay collecting on the greater of the couple's individual benefits.

Child in care benefits at any age

The spouse of a fully insured worked can also receive (only) the spouse's benefit at any age if he or she is caring for a child of the worker who is also receiving benefits. The spouse's benefit would continue until the worker's child reaches age 16. At that time, the child's benefits continue, but the spouse's benefits stop unless he or she is old enough to receive benefits based on his or her own age.

Benefits for an ex-spouse

Note: This election for ex-spouse benefits is available only to those people born in 1953 and earlier.

With divorce, the ex-spouse of a fully insured worker can receive benefits based on the former spouse's earnings even if the insured worker remarries. For benefits to be available to an ex-spouse, certain requirements must be satisfied:

- The marriage lasted 10 years or longer.
- The ex-spouse remains unmarried through age 60.

- The ex-spouse is age 62 or older.
- The benefit that the ex-spouse is entitled to receive based on his or her own work is less than the benefit he or she would receive based on the former spouse's FICA earnings.
- The former spouse is eligible for Social Security retirement or disability benefits.

If the spouse on whose earnings the benefits are based has not applied for retirement benefits, but is qualified for them, then the ex-spouse can receive benefits on former spouse's record if the divorce was finalized two or more years prior to the ex-spouse applying for benefits. If the divorced spouse remarries, he or she generally cannot collect benefits on the former spouse's earnings record unless his or her subsequent marriage ends (whether by death, divorce, or annulment). Of course, if the ex-spouse is eligible for retirement benefits on his or her own record, the Social Security retirement benefit may be that amount. However, if the benefit on the former spouse's earnings record is a higher amount, the ex will receive benefits reflecting that higher amount (reduced for age).

Once a divorced spouse has reached full retirement age and is eligible for a spouse's benefit and his or her own retirement benefit, he or she has a choice. A divorced spouse can elect to receive *only the divorced spouse's benefits* when he or she applies online and, therefore, delay receiving retirement benefits until a later date. If his or her retirement benefits are delayed, a higher benefit may be received later based on the effect of delayed retirement credits.

An ex-spouse collecting benefits based on the former spouse's work record does not affect the benefits of the former spouse or the benefits of the former spouse's new spouse.

Earned income limitations

If the former spouse continues to work while receiving benefits, the same earnings limits apply to him or her as apply to the former spouse on whose earnings the retirement benefits are based.

If an ex-spouse will also receive a pension based on work not covered by Social Security, such as government or foreign work, his or her Social Security benefit record may be affected.

Mini case

Arguably, the reason why Andy Fletcher, now 66, has been married four times is his quick temper. He is currently married to Sue. Sue is very attractive and considerably younger than Andy. Andy's first wife, Mary, died in an auto accident 27 years ago. Andy's second wife, Cynthia, remarried 11 years ago after being married to Andy for 10 1/2 years characterized by arguments. Andy's third wife, Patience (she ran out of hers) divorced him after a rocky 12-year marriage.

As his current wife, Sue would be entitled to spousal Social Security retirement benefits, as would Patience because she was married to Andy for longer than 10 years. Cynthia having remarried would not be entitled to a spousal Social Security retirement benefit based on Andy's earnings.

Benefits for children of retirees

When a fully insured worker qualifies for Social Security retirement benefits, his or her children may also qualify to receive benefits based on the parent's FICA earnings. An eligible child can be the worker's biological child, adopted child, or stepchild. A dependent grandchild may also qualify.

To receive benefits, the child must be

- unmarried; and
- under age 18; or
- 18–19 years old and a full-time student (no higher than grade 12); or
- 18 or older and disabled from a disability that started before age 22.

> ### Example 3-10
>
> Hillary Mann's mother is eligible for Social Security retirement benefits. Hillary turns age 18 in November 2018 but will not graduate from high school until June 2019. Hillary's benefits would continue through June 2019.

Normally, benefits stop when children reach age 18 unless they are disabled. However, if the child is still a full-time student at a secondary (or elementary) school at age 18, benefits will continue until the child graduates or until two months after the child becomes age 19, whichever is first.

Benefits paid to a worker's child do not decrease either the worker's or the spouse's retirement benefit. Keep in mind, however, that a maximum family benefit amount applies. Also, the qualifying parent must be receiving a benefit for the child to receive a benefit.

When are benefits actually paid?

Social Security benefits are paid the month after they are due. A worker who applies for benefits in May will receive the first check in June. Further, although the check will not arrive until June, the worker must be eligible for the benefit as of the time of the application, in this case, May.

Electronic payments

Rules that took effect in 2013 require that all Social Security and SSI benefits be received electronically. Individuals who apply for benefits now do so electronically. Individuals who have been receiving benefits by check will be contacted by the Treasury Department to arrange for electronic filing. Those already receiving benefits may create a *"my* Social Security" account and initiate (or change) direct deposit online.

Only one account

Currently, the system allows only for electronic transfer to one (typically bank) account. However, once the bank receives the funds, the bank itself may provide arrangements for the deposit to be split among accounts.

Benefit recipients living abroad

The SSA will transfer benefit payments to foreign banks only if the foreign country in which the U.S. citizen is now residing has an international direct deposit agreement with the United States.

Waiving out of electronic transfer

Given the constraints of certain older Americans, the Treasury recognizes that under rare circumstances electronic payment is not viable, and it will provide a waiver.

Treasury can grant exceptions in rare circumstances. For more information or to request a waiver, call Treasury at 855-290-1545. You may also print and fill out a waiver form and return it to the address on the form. (See https://www.ssa.gov/deposit/ for waiver form.)

Maximum family benefit

The maximum family benefit is the maximum monthly amount that can be paid on a worker's earnings record. There is a special formula for computing the maximum benefits payable to the family of a disabled worker. The following, however, is devoted to the more common family maximum for retirement and survivor benefits.

Family benefits—spousal benefits, survivor, mother or father, and children benefits—are called auxiliary benefits. The total family maximum benefit amount each year is the wage earner's personal maximum plus the maximum of auxiliary benefits for family members. Benefits based on a worker's FICA earnings paid to a former spouse are not considered in calculating the maximum family benefit. The maximum benefit that the family, including the worker, can receive also depends on when the worker first claims Social Security retirement benefits.

Generally, the maximum family benefit has no impact on two spouses collecting Social Security retirement benefits on their respective earnings. It is when there are children and other dependents that the family maximum benefit is most likely to become an issue.

Generally, the maximum family benefit represents between 150% and 180% of the worker's full retirement benefit.

Beware early benefits

If the worker takes retirement benefits early, the retirement benefit will (in the absence of any withdrawal) be permanently reduced. Let's say that Howard Garner needs cash flow now and claims his Social Security retirement benefit at age 62 resulting in a 25% cut from the amount that would have been his PIA-based benefit at his full or normal retirement age of 66.

In that light, the maximum family benefit available to the Garner family based on Howard's FICA earnings is 75% of Howard's PIA and 50 percent in auxiliary benefits. Sadly, this translates to only 125% of what might have been Howard's full PIA.

Delaying retirement benefits pays off

Contrast Howard Garner's situation (and that of his family) with that of his brother, Gerald Garner. Unlike Howard, the more financially successful Gerald did not have a pressing need for cash from Social Security retirement benefits and is able to delay claiming his benefit until the cap age of 70.

Because of the delayed retirement credit, Gerald's monthly retirement benefit now represents 132% of his full retirement age PIA. Therefore, the auxiliary benefits will represent 187 of the amount of Gerald's PIA at his FRA or NRA.

Computation of the retirement and survivor family maximum

The formula used to compute the family maximum is similar to the formula used to compute the PIA. The formula sums four separate percentages of portions of the worker's PIA. For 2019, these portions are the first $1,184, the amount between $1,184 and $1,708, the amount between $1,708 and $2,228, and the amount greater than $2,228. These dollar amounts are the "bend points" of the family-maximum formula. Therefore, the family-maximum bend points for 2018 are $1,144, $1,651, and $2,154. See the table showing bend points for years beginning with 1979. (The table also shows PIA formula bend points.)

For the family of a worker who becomes age 62 or dies in 2019 before attaining age 62, the total amount of benefits payable will be computed so that it does not exceed

a.   150% of the first $1,184 of the worker's PIA, plus
b.   272% of the worker's PIA greater than $1,184 through $1,708, plus
c.   134% of the worker's PIA greater than $1,708 through $2,228, plus
d.   175% of the worker's PIA greater than $2,228.

We then round this total amount to the next lower multiple of $0.10 if it is not already a multiple of $0.10.

The maximum family benefit is the maximum monthly amount that can be paid on a worker's earnings record. There is a special formula for computing the maximum benefits payable to the family of a disabled worker. The family maximum for a family of a disabled worker is 85% of the worker's AIME. However, it cannot be less than the worker's PIA nor more than 150% of the PIA.

Example 3-11

Agatha is a low-income worker who claims Social Security retirement benefits at the first opportunity, at age 62, because she needs the money for her basic living expenses. Her FRA is age 66. Her retirement benefit will be reduced permanently to 75% of what she would have received at her full retirement age. The maximum benefit she and her family can receive is 75% of Agatha's PIA (her reduced retirement benefit) plus 50% of her PIA in auxiliary benefits. In this case, Agatha's family maximum is only 125%—75% plus 50%—of her full retirement benefit.

Now, let us look at Allen Woods who waits until his full retirement age to claim benefits. He would have a family benefit maximum equal to 187% of his full PIA.

Finally, consider, Fred who can afford to wait until he turns age 70 to collect his retirement benefit. In this situation, his own retirement benefit is 1.32 times his PIA due to the "delayed retirement credit" and the maximum auxiliary benefits are 87% of his PIA.

Once the family has reached the maximum benefit amount, benefits will be reduced for the auxiliary beneficiaries proportionately but not for the FICA wage earner's benefit. Further, if a dependent in a family who has reached the maximum stops receiving benefits (for example, a dependent child finishes high school or marries), reductions to other auxiliary beneficiaries would be increased accordingly.

Working after retirement

Many older Americans need or choose to work during their traditional retirement years. Working during one's 60s may reduce a worker's Social Security retirement benefit.

Consider earned income limits

A worker does not have to be retired to claim Social Security retirement benefits. However, if the benefit recipient continues to work and earns amounts of earned income exceeding inflation-indexed thresholds, all or part of the retirement benefits may be temporarily withheld. Certainly, investment income and retirement plan distributions are not considered to be earned income for this purpose, nor are workers' compensation or unemployment insurance benefits. Wages, salaries, tips, and net self-employment earnings are treated as earned income for this purpose.

Before full retirement age

Workers under their full retirement age can earn up to $17,640 without penalty in 2018 and $17,040 without penalty in 2018. When earned income exceeds this inflation-indexed threshold, the Social Security retirement benefit recipient loses $1 in benefits for every $2 by which earned income exceeds the threshold.

Example 3-12

Ruth Sanders' full retirement age is 66, which occurs in August of 2019. In 2018, her earned income from working was $25,040, which exceeded the 2018 threshold of $17,040 by $8,000. Presume that her annual benefit is $9,600 representing monthly payments of $800. The SSA would reduce Ruth's benefit by $4,000. She would still receive an annual Social Security retirement benefit of $5,600.

The full or normal retirement age year

In the year in which a fully insured worker reaches his or her normal retirement age, the earnings limit increases to $46,920 in 2019 (it was $45,360 in 2018), and the penalty is reduced to 33 cents withheld from each dollar of earned income above the limit. Continuing with the example of Ruth Sanders, now presume year 2019. In 2019, Ruth earns $60,000 in the workplace. From January 2019 through July 2019, Ruth had earned income of $47,970. Ruth would experience a benefit reduction of $350, losing 33 cents of benefit for each dollar by which her earned income exceeds the threshold, but considering only her earned income up to her full retirement age. Once Ruth attains her FRA, the benefit reduction for earned income disappears.

Clients with high-paying jobs can easily wipe out benefits—which makes a strong argument for delaying benefits until after the NRA.

After the full or normal retirement year

Under the Freedom to Work Act, after a worker's Social Security retirement benefit reaches his or her full retirement age, there is no penalty for working and claiming benefits at the same time. This begins in the month in which the worker attains the FRA.

Benefit reduction is not permanent

Benefits are not permanently withheld. The money deducted from Social Security retirement benefits when a worker has earned income over the limit is not withheld forever. Once that worker reaches his or her full retirement age, benefits are recalculated to provide a credit corresponding to the reduced benefits.

Example 3-13

Anthony Alden is a 62-year-old worker who claims $800 a month in Social Security benefits and earns $25,640 annually from working until age 66. He would have $4,000, or five months' worth of benefits, withheld from his Social Security checks over the course of the year because of the earnings limit. When he reaches age 66, Anthony's full retirement age, his monthly benefit amount will increase to $895 to give him credit for the 20 months of withheld benefits.

Potentially higher FICA wages in one's 60s

Social Security retirement benefits are calculated based on a worker's 35 highest years of earnings. If one of a fully insured worker's highest earnings years happens after benefit payments begin, that worker's payments will automatically increase the following year. Earnings of a fully insured worker that are lower than the earlier computed top 35 years will not reduce the worker's benefit.

Summary

Social Security retirement benefits contribute to the incomes of more than 67 million Americans. The amount of those benefits, presuming that the worker is fully insured, depends on the worker's AIME, his or her PIA, and when that worker first claims retirement benefits. Under certain formulas, monthly benefit payments are reduced for retiring prior to the normal retirement age and are increased for delaying benefits claims until after the normal retirement age. In years before and including the normal or full retirement year, benefits will be reduced if the claimant's earned income exceeds specified thresholds. Retirement benefits are also available to spouses (even divorced spouses) and children of eligible workers if certain requirements are met. Historically, Social Security retirement benefits have been increased most years for inflation.

Of course, the rules for Social Security retirement benefits may change in the future. Given that the CPA is often the client's most trusted source for financial guidance, the CPA should keep abreast of developments related to Social Security benefits. Check www.ssa.gov for the latest rates and information.

Knowledge checks

1. Howard was born in 1970. His FRA or NRA is

   a. Age 60.
   b. Age 65.
   c. Age 66.
   d. Age 67.

2. Clark's FRA or NRA is age 66. He decides to claim his Social Security retirement benefits at age 62. Which statement best describes the effect of Clark's decision on his benefits?

   a. Clark's benefit will not be affected because age 62 is a permissible age for claiming Social Security retirement benefits.
   b. Clark's retirement benefit will be reduced by $5/9$ of 1% for each month of benefits paid before his FRA or NRA for 36 months and 5/12 of 1% for 12 months.
   c. Clark's retirement benefit will be reduced by $5/12$ of 1% for each month of benefits paid before his FRA or NRA.
   d. Clark's benefit will be reduced to 50% of his PIA.

3. Clara Bowen worked as a part-time assistant librarian for more than 20 years. Her PIA is $800 per month. Her husband, Robert, worked as a radiologist in a major hospital. His PIA is $2,200 per month. Presuming that Clara claims benefits at her FRA or NRA, which of the following statements is true?

   a. Clara can claim the combination of her benefits and her spousal benefits for a total of $3,000 per month.
   b. Because Clara is fully insured she may claim benefits based only on her own earnings.
   c. Clara may claim 50% of Robert's PIA because it is higher than her own benefit.
   d. Clara would receive 37.5% of Robert's benefits.

4. All but which are correct with respect to Social Security benefits?

   a. Actuarially, the SSA has determined that the average person would benefit by delaying his or her Social Security distribution to age 69.
   b. Social Security benefits are increased if a fully insured worker delays retirement beyond full retirement age.
   c. Most older Americans choose to take Social Security retirement benefits at their normal retirement age.
   d. The earliest age a fully covered worker can begin getting Social Security retirement benefits is 62.

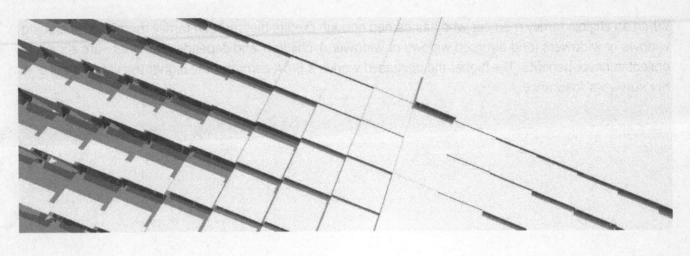

Chapter 4

Social Security Survivors' Benefits

Learning objectives

- Recognize the types of situations that may jeopardize a widow's or widower's survivor benefits.

- Identify the special considerations for disabled widows or widowers, and younger spouses taking care of children.

- Recall the amount of benefit available to a widow or widower based on decedent's primary insurance amount (PIA).

- Recognize the types of Social Security benefits that are available to widows and widowers.

- Identify situations in which a grandchild may be eligible for survivor benefits based on a grandparent's Social Security credits.

Overview

Social Security survivors' benefits—based on a deceased worker's Federal Insurance Contributions Act (FICA) earnings—are, if certain requirements are satisfied, paid to their surviving widows or widowers, their surviving minor and disabled children, and even their dependent parents. A surviving spouse who has not reached the minimum age requirement for widow's benefits may still be entitled to a mother's or father's benefit if caring for a minor or disabled child of the deceased spouse. The amount of the benefit is based on the deceased worker's work history, rather than on the benefit recipient's workplace earnings.

When an eligible family member who has earned enough credits dies, certain family members—including widows or widowers (and divorced widows or widowers), children, and dependent parents—are eligible to collect survivor benefits. The higher the deceased worker's FICA earnings, the higher the value of his or her survivors' insurance.

No benefits in the month of death

No benefits are payable the month that a beneficiary dies. The Social Security check received in the month a retirement benefit recipient has died should be returned to the Social Security Administration (SSA). Methods for returning the check differ depending on whether the check is direct deposited or mailed.

If Social Security benefit checks are being direct deposited, which is generally the case, a family member of the decedent or the decedent's executor should notify the bank as soon as possible. If the check arrives in the mail, it should be taken to the local Social Security office to have the payee's name changed.

Survivor benefit eligibility

The following individuals are generally eligible for Social Security survivor benefits, presuming the deceased family member had earned sufficient credits or quarters of coverage to qualify:

- Widow or widower who has not remarried before age 60 (If an individual remarries prior to age 60, survivor benefits are not available in most cases.)
    - At any age, if caring for children younger than 16 or disabled children who get benefits
    - If born before 1938, full benefits at age 65 or older, or reduced benefits at age 60
    - If born after 1960, full benefits at age 67 or older or reduced benefits at age 60
    - If disabled, benefits at age 50–60
- Unmarried children
    - If younger than age 18
    - If younger than age 19 and in elementary or secondary school (not college)
    - If disabled before age 22 and remains disabled
    - Adopted children, grandchildren, or stepchildren under certain conditions
- Dependent parents
    - Age 62 or older

Knowledge check

1. When Tom Harding died at a relatively young age, he had enough credits for survivor benefits. Who among his four children would be eligible for child's benefits?

    a. Kim, age 18, a college freshman.
    b. Tim, age 18, who recently married.
    c. Jim, age 18½, a high school senior.
    d. Slim, age 20, a high school senior.

Reduction for early requests

The survivor benefit is generally equal to the deceased worker's benefit amount (if he or she was collecting benefits at death). Keep in mind, however, that it may be reduced depending upon the surviving spouse's age.

This is similar to the reduction applied to regular retirement benefits. Note, however, that spousal survivor benefits can be claimed as early as age 60, rather than age 62 as for retirement benefits (and as early as age 50 for a disabled surviving spouse).

At age 60, the survivor benefit is reduced to 71.5% for all dates of birth, in addition to the fact that the survivor benefit can be received two years earlier than earliest retirement age of 62, the table for full retirement age (FRA) is adjusted by two years.

Example 4-1

Francis Flanagan can claim retirement benefits as early as age 62. Her FRA retirement benefits would begin at age 66. However, she would be entitled to 100% of her late husband's benefit as early as 64.

Logically, when the deceased spouse was receiving retirement benefits, any reductions or increases that had been applied also factor into the survivor benefit. Taking retirement benefits early can permanently reduce any survivor benefit that the surviving spouse might receive.

In contrast, if the deceased spouse was not already receiving retirement benefits the month of his or her death, the first factor is the amount that the decedent would have received at the final attained age, (based on date of birth) if he or she were still living.

If the deceased spouse would have been younger than his or her full or normal retirement age when the surviving spouse files for benefits, the first factor must be reduced from the PIA. Similarly, if the deceased spouse would have been older than full or normal retirement age when the survivor benefit is applied for, the benefit will be increased from the primary insurance amount.

Year of birth	60	61	62	63	64	65	66	67
1939 or before	−28.5%	−22.8%	−17.1%	−11.4%	−5.7%	0.0%		
1940	−28.5%	−23.0%	−17.5%	−12.0%	−6.4%	−0.9%		
1941	−28.5%	−23.2%	−17.8%	−12.5%	−7.1%	−1.8%		
1942	−28.5%	−23.3%	−18.1%	−13.0%	−7.8%	−2.6%		
1943	−28.5%	−23.5%	−18.4%	−13.4%	−8.4%	−3.4%		
1944	−28.5%	−23.6%	−18.7%	−13.8%	−9.0%	−4.1%		
1945 to 1956	−28.5%	−23.7%	−19.0%	−14.2%	−9.5%	−4.7%	0.0%	
1957	−28.5%	−23.9%	−19.3%	−14.6%	−10.0%	−5.4%	−0.8%	
1958	−28.5%	−24.0%	−19.5%	−15.0%	−10.5%	−6.0%	−1.5%	
1959	−28.5%	−24.1%	−19.7%	−15.3%	−11.0%	−6.6%	−2.2%	
1960	−28.5%	−24.2%	−19.9%	−15.7%	−11.4%	−7.1%	−2.8%	
1961	−28.5%	−24.3%	−20.2%	−16.0%	−11.8%	−7.6%	−3.5%	
1962 or later	−28.5%	−24.4%	−20.4%	−16.3%	−12.2%	−8.1%	−4.1%	0.0%

Source: www.socialsecurity.gov
Note that in this chart, the *year of birth* refers to that of the survivor rather than the decedent.

At the survivor's age 60, the reduction is 28.5% for all dates of birth. Then the reduction factor is eliminated gradually up through the survivor benefit FRA.

Calculating widow's or widower's benefits

To calculate the amount of the widow's or widower's benefit, apply the reduction factor to the survivor benefit.

Example 4-2

Peter Goodman's PIA would have been $1,500, and his widow, Sally Goodman, is 62 years old. If Sally were to take the survivor benefit now, the $1,500 will be reduced by 19.0% to $1,215. (See the preceding table.) Sally is now 62, meaning she was born in 1953 or 1954. Waiting another four years before claiming survivor benefit would enable Sally to receive the full benefit with no reduction, plus any cost-of-living adjustments (COLAs) that would be applied to the first factor during the four years during which she delayed benefits.

Remarriage may jeopardize benefits

If the surviving spouse has remarried before age 60, the survivor benefit is no longer available. However, if the surviving spouse remarries before age 60 and then subsequently divorces or is subsequently widowed again, the survivor benefit is available again.

If the surviving spouse has more than one deceased spouse, he or she is eligible to receive survivor benefits based upon the highest possible benefit from any but not all of the prior spouses, as long as they were married for at least 10 years.

Example 4-3

Lucinda was married first to Mack, for 12 years, and later, after age 60, to Jack. Mack was a very successful real estate agent. Jack was a far less financially successful part-time entertainer. Lucinda would receive benefits based on Mack's PIA even though she was married to Jack when Mack died.

Switching from widow's or widower's benefits to retirement benefits

If a widow or widower is receiving benefits based on the FICA earnings of his or her late spouse, that widow or widower may, at a later date, switch to his or her own (retirement) benefit as early as age 62.

This would make sense if the widow's own retirement benefit was of a greater amount than the survivor's benefit.

It is not unusual for a widow or widower to begin to receive a survivor benefit at a reduced rate then later switch to one not exposed to reduction. The Bipartisan Budget Bill of 2015 did not change the rules in the case of death. A widow or widower is still allowed to claim the survivor benefit only, rather than his or her own and then switch to his or her own benefit at a later date.

Parental benefits for significantly younger widows or widowers

There is also a survivor benefit available for a (potentially) much younger surviving spouse if that survivor is caring for a child aged 16 or younger. This benefit is equal to 100% of the benefit that the decedent-spouse was receiving at his or her death, or the primary insurance amount to which he or she was entitled, if he or she was not currently receiving benefits at death.

Any benefits require that the deceased spouse earned adequate Social Security quarters or credits. For full benefits, the deceased would need to have earned at least 40 quarters, or 10 years of work. For the surviving spouse caring for a child younger than age 16, reduced benefits are available if the deceased spouse had earned at least six quarters of credit in the three years prior to his or her death. Any amount of quarters between the minimum of six and the maximum of 40, results in a phased increase in the benefit amount.

The general rule is that to qualify for this benefit that the surviving spouse had to have been married to the deceased spouse for at least nine months. However, an exception is available if the deceased worker died within three months of an accident or died while on active duty in the armed services.

Having a "child in care" is a basic requirement for some benefits, including spouse's benefits for a spouse younger than age 62 and for mother's and father's benefits. According to the SSA, in care means

- exercising parental control and responsibility for the welfare and care of a child younger than age 16 or a mentally disabled child aged 16 or older; or
- performing personal services for a physically disabled child aged 16 or older.

The mother or father may exercise parental control and responsibility or perform personal services alone or with another. When the child in care turns 16, the parent may continue to receive benefits if the child is disabled and the parent meets the requirements for having a disabled child in care.

> **Example 4-4**
>
> When Irene Stanton's husband died, she was aged 39 and caring for their twin girls, Lillie and Billie, who were age 11. Although Irene is clearly younger than age 60 (the first opportunity to claim widow's benefits), she would be entitled to a benefit of 75% of her late husband's PIA if he was fully insured. The daughters, Lillie and Billie, would also be entitled to a benefit of 75% each.

Knowledge check

2. According to the Social Security Administration, what does it mean to have a child in care?

    a. The deceased worker's widow or widower is exercising parental control and responsibility for the welfare and care of a child younger than age 16 or a physically or mentally disabled child aged 16 or older.
    b. The deceased worker's widow or widower maintains constant supervision over the deceased's child younger than age 16 or a physically or mentally disabled child aged 16 or older.
    c. The deceased worker's widow or widower is supporting the educational needs of the deceased's child younger than age 16 or a physically or mentally disabled child aged 16 or older.
    d. The deceased worker's widow or widower personally provides all physical care for the deceased's child younger than age 16 or a physically or mentally disabled child aged 16 or older.

Disabled widows or widowers

The disabled widow or widower of a worker with sufficient Social Security quarters or credits is entitled to receive survivor benefits based on the deceased spouse's work record. The applicant must be between the ages of 50 and 60 with a medical condition that satisfies the SSA's definition of disability for adults. The widow or widower disability must have begun before or within seven years of the deceased spouse's death.

This seven-year period is adjusted if the disabled widow or widower is also receiving Social Security mother's or father's benefits. In this case, the disabled surviving spouse may still be eligible for disabled widow or widower benefits if his or her disability had begun before the mother or father's benefits end or within seven years after they end.

Strict definition of disability

The definition of disability under Social Security is different than that used in commercially issued disability income insurance policies. Social Security pays only for total disability. Benefits are not available for partial disability or for short-term disability.

Disability under Social Security is based on one's inability to work. An individual is considered disabled under Social Security rules if

- he or she can no longer perform the work that he or she did before the disability began;
- the SSA deemed that the widow or widower cannot adjust to other work because of medical condition(s); and
- the individual's disability has lasted or is expected to last for at least one year or to result in death.

This is a harsh definition of disability. Social Security presumes that working families have access to other income resources during periods of short-term disabilities, including workers' compensation, insurance, savings, and investments.

Just as with other Social Security survivor benefits, benefit amount payable to a disabled widow or widower is based on a percentage of the deceased spouse's PIA rather than on the earnings of the widow or widower's work record. For a disabled widow or widower, the monthly amount is generally around 71½% of the deceased spouse's PIA.

Remarriage

Remarriage can affect survivor benefit eligibility. The general rule is if a widow or widower remarries before she or he reaches age 60 (age 50 if disabled), he or she cannot receive Social Security benefits as a surviving spouse while married. If remarriage occurs after age 60 (age 50 if disabled), SSA survivor benefits can continue if the survivor was born in 1953 or earlier.

The lump-sum Social Security death benefit

In addition to ongoing survivor benefits, Social Security pays a small lump-sum death benefit of $255.

The Social Security lump-sum death benefit is available to

- the spouse of the deceased insured worker who is living in the same household, or
- the dependent child of the deceased worker who is eligible to receive Social Security benefits based on the worker's earnings record.

Mini case

Gwen Varner's husband Leonard died recently. They had two children—Cathy and Carrie, ages 11 and 14, respectively. Gwen's father, Sidney, a long-time widower, has been in poor health. Sidney is now 88 years old.

She could claim the lump-sum death benefit based on Leonard's earnings.

Now assume that both Gwen and Leonard were killed in an auto accident. The children could claim the (one) $255 death benefit.

Gwen's father, Sidney, just died. Because he has no living spouse or dependent children, the lump-sum death benefit will not be paid.

The lump-sum death benefit is payable as long as the deceased worker was currently insured, meaning that they had at least six quarters of earnings covered by Social Security withholding during the full 13-quarter period prior to his or her death.

This tiny amount has been regarded by Social Security as a funeral benefit. Obviously, the amount has not been indexed for inflation.

Applying for the benefit

If the Social Security death benefit is being paid to a widow or widower who is receiving spouse's benefit, then no application for the lump-sum death benefit needs be filed.

If the Social Security death benefit is being paid to an eligible dependent child, then an application must be filed within two years of the insured worker's death.

General rules for claiming survivor benefits

The manner in which individuals request survivor benefits differently depends on whether they already receive benefits from Social Security.

An application for an ongoing monthly Social Security death benefit should be filed within six months of the worker's death. This is because no more than six months' worth of benefits will be paid retroactively.

If an individual is not currently receiving benefits from Social Security, he or she should

- immediately apply for survivor benefits by telephone, online or at a local Social Security office; and
- supply the SSA with original or certified copies of
    - proof of death—notice from the funeral home or a death certificate;
    - his or her Social Security number, as well as the deceased's Social Security number;
    - his or her birth certificate;
    - his or her marriage certificate if he or she is the widow or widower;
    - his or her divorce papers if applying as a divorced spouse;
    - the Social Security numbers of all dependent children;
    - the most recent W-2 form or federal self-employment tax return of the deceased; and
    - his or her bank name and account number.

If the applicant is already receiving Social Security Benefits, he or she should

- immediately report the death so that benefit payments on the spouse's record can be changed to survivor benefits, and
- contact a Social Security representative to discuss whether his or her own benefits or survivor benefits will result in larger benefit payments.

Children's benefits

Social Security benefits millions of children. According to the SSA, about 4.1 million children lived in a household receiving Social Security benefits.[1]

Mini case

Charles Belkin died when he was fully insured. Charles' PIA was $1,500 per month. His son Jason is 16 and earned around $9,000 in the past year or so installing and troubleshooting computers for friends and neighbors. Jason is an athletically-minded junior at Kennedy High School.

Jason's survivor benefit would represent 75% of his father's PIA amounting to $1,125 per month. His survivor benefits would be tax free. However, if Jason's mother, grandparents, or other siblings are also getting benefits on his father's record, his benefits might be reduced. The SSA limits the amount a family can get on one worker's record to between 150% and 180% of his PIA. If the total family benefits did exceed the limit, each person's benefit payments are reduced proportionately.

Although Jason does have earned income, the amount is comfortably less than the $17,640 threshold that would trigger a reduction in his survivor benefit.

Perhaps in the future, Jason's benefits might become income taxable to him. Let us also say that Jason soon begins receiving an income distribution of $30,000 annually from a trust fund that was established at his father's death. Jason's benefits will become taxable because his provisional income, which includes his income plus half of his survivor benefits exceed income limits set by the IRS. Jason's (because he is only 16, we will presume that he is single,) provisional income was $36,750 (more than the $34,000 second base amount). Because the provisional income exceeds $34,000, 85% of the excess amount is included in income.

Grandchildren

It is possible for grandchildren to receive survivor benefits based on a grandparent's earnings record. For this purpose, step-grandchildren are treated as grandchildren. To receive these survivor benefits, all the following requirements must be met:

- The parents of the grandchild must be deceased or disabled.
- The grandchild began living with the grandparent before he or she turned 18 years old.
- The grandchild received at least half of his or her support from the grandparent in the year before the grandparent died.
- If the grandchild is younger than 12 months old, it must be shown that he or she lived with the grandparent and received at least half of his or her support from the grandparent since birth.

---

[1] Source: SSA.gov; https://www.ssa.gov/pubs/EN-05-10085.pdf

If the grandchild is formally adopted by the grandparents, they do not need to meet the previously listed requirements. Instead, they must meet the requirements that apply to children (of a parent).

Example 4-5

After both of her parents died suddenly in a boating accident, Edith Simon lived with her grandmother, Gladys Simon. Grandma Gladys died when Edith was 13. Grandma Gladys had been fully insured at the time of her death. Edith will be entitled to benefits based on Grandma Gladys' PIA, generally at 75%. Therefore, if Grandma Gladys' PIA had been $1,000 per month, Edith's survivor benefit would be $750 per month. Had Grandma Gladys not earned 40 credits or quarters, Edith's benefits would be smaller.

Knowledge check

3. Based on a deceased worker's survivor benefits, how far back may retroactive payments to survivors go?

    a. Three months.
    b. Six months.
    c. Nine months.
    d. Eighteen months.

Dependent parent's benefits

Social Security survivor benefits may be available for dependent parents of eligible workers. To qualify for the program, the parent must

- be at least age 62;
- have not married after the deceased worker's death (unless an exception applies);
- received at least one-half of his or her support from the deceased worker at certain points in time;
- have filed proof of support with the SSA within the required time limit; and
- not be entitled to a higher Social Security retirement benefit on his or her own work record.

Benefit amounts recap

Typically, the amount that the beneficiary will receive is a percentage of the deceased's PIA includes the following:

- A widow or widower older than 66 years will generally receive 100% of the deceased's PIA.
- A widow or widower aged 60–64 years will generally receive a benefit close to 71%–94% of his or her deceased spouse's PIA.
- A disabled widow or widower aged 50–59 years will generally receive a benefit of 71% of his or her deceased spouse's PIA.
- Widows and widowers with children younger than age 16 will receive 75% of the deceased spouse's PIA at any age.
- Eligible children of the deceased worker will generally receive a benefit representing 75% of the deceased parent's PIA.

Summary

In this section, we have explored various benefits available under Social Security to survivors of deceased workers who, at death, were currently or fully insured. Widow's or widower's benefits, albeit reduced, are available as early as the surviving spouse aged 60, or up to 10 years younger for a disabled widow or widower. Survivor benefits are also available to divorced spouses, following a marriage to the deceased worker that had lasted at least 10 years. Remarriage may disqualify the widow or widower from survivor benefits under certain circumstances. The amount of the benefit is pegged to the deceased worker's PIA rather than the widow's or widower's. Survivor benefits are also available to minor children of the deceased worker if they are in elementary or high school, but not college. Survivor benefits may be available to elderly, dependent parents of a deceased worker if they do not have meaningful Social Security benefits of their own. A family maximum benefit generally applies.

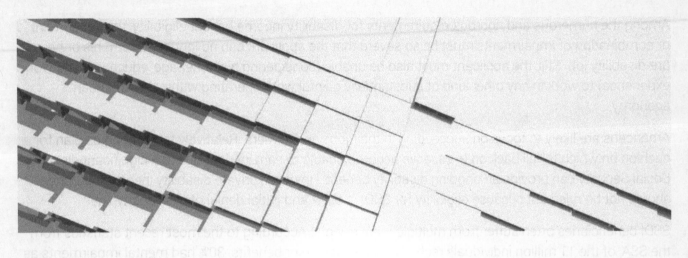

Chapter 5

Disability Income Benefits

Learning objectives

- Recall the relationship between Social Security disability income benefits and retirement benefits.

- Identify how claims for Social Security disability income benefits are made.

- Recognize the relationship between Social Security disability income benefits and Medicare.

- Recall how Supplemental Security Income (SSI) operates.

Overview

An individual's chances of becoming disabled are greater than most people think. Studies conducted by the Social Security Administration (SSA) show that a 20-year-old worker has a 3-in-10 chance of becoming disabled before reaching his or her full retirement age.

Social Security disability insurance, or SSDI, is a federally operated and regulated disability insurance program. Workers pay for this federal insurance through Federal Insurance Contribution Acts (FICA) taxes. SSDI is distinct from Medicare, Medicaid, and the needs-based SSI programs. SSDI provides monthly benefits to eligible workers who have not attained their full or normal retirement ages (65–67) and can no longer work because of a significant disability that is expected to last 12 months or more, or is expected to be terminal. As in the case of other types of Social Security benefits, the SSDI benefit is based on the recipient's FICA-covered earnings history. However, benefit limits are substantially lower.

Among the numerous and rigorous requirements for disability income benefit eligibility, the impairment or combination of impairments must be so severe that the applicant can no longer perform his or her pre-disability job. Still, the applicant must also be unable (considering his or her age, education, and work experience) to work in any other kind of substantially gainful work operating within the American economy.

Americans are likely to focus on succeeding in their jobs and careers. Relatively few among us plan for a cushion on which to fall back on in case we become unable to earn income due to a significant disability. Social Security can provide an ongoing disability benefit. However, private disability income insurance should not be ruled out because eligibility for SSDI is strict and initial denial of claims is typical.

SSDI beneficiaries often suffer from multiple impairments. According to the most recent statistics from the SSA, of the 11 million individuals receiving disabled worker benefits, 30% had mental impairments as the main disabling condition (primary diagnosis). They include 10% with schizophrenia and 20% with other mental disorders. Musculoskeletal conditions such as arthritis, back injuries, and other disorders of the skeleton and connective tissues were classified as the primary diagnosis for 32% of the workers receiving Social Security disability benefits.

Musculoskeletal conditions were more prevalent among beneficiaries over age 50. Approximately 8% claimed benefits from disabilities were pegged to heart disease or circulatory diseases. Another 10% suffered impairments of the nervous system and sense organs. The remaining 20% include those with injuries, cancers, infectious diseases, metabolic and endocrine diseases, such as diabetes, diseases of the respiratory system and diseases of other body systems.

Characteristics attributable to disabled-worker beneficiaries

Disabled-worker beneficiaries face unpleasant economic challenges. About 34% of disabled workers versus 13% of other working age adults have incomes less than 125% of the poverty threshold.

SSDI recipients are also more likely to be older, with the average age of beneficiaries at 53. Within this group, almost 70% are over 50 years old whereas about 30% are over 60 years old. Many recipients would be considered as terminally ill. Approximately 20% of male beneficiaries and one in seven female beneficiaries die within the first five years after receiving their first disability income benefit from Social Security.

Determining the benefit

The amount of the monthly SSDI benefit is based on a weighted formula that the Social Security Administration applies to calculate benefits for each approved applicant. Social Security bases both retirement and disability benefits on the amount of FICA income attributable to the covered worker, the so-called "covered earnings." As with retirement benefits, the formula consists of fixed percentages of different amounts of income (called "bend points," which are adjusted each year).

Bend point mini case

Recall that bend points represent portions of a worker's average annual FICA income (average indexed monthly earnings or AIME) in specific dollar amounts indexed each year, based upon the average wage index (AWI) series.

It is noteworthy that AWI figures are always two years in arrears. Therefore, the AWI figure used to determine the 2019 bend points is based on 2017 wage averages.

The bend points for 2019 are $926 and $5,583.

Here is how this applies:

Matt Kincaid becomes eligible for SSDI benefits in 2019. His AIME is $6,500. Ninety percent of the first $926 of his AIME is included in his primary insurance amount (PIA), plus 32% of his AIME from $926 to $5,583 plus 15% of Matt's AIME over $5,583. The amounts are added up to determine Matt's PIA as follows:

$926 \times .90 =$	$833.40
+ $4,657 \times .32 =$	$1,490.24
+ $917 \times .15 =$	$137.55
Matt's PIA	**$2,461.19**

(Per the preceding calculation, $5,583 − $926 = $4,657; and $6,500 − $5,583 = $917.)

Relationship between retirement and disability income benefits

Generally, a worker may not receive Social Security retirement benefits and disability benefits at the same time. SSDI operates to provide disability benefits to disabled individuals who are too young to receive Social Security old age (retirement) benefits.

An exception

There is, however, an exception when an individual draws less than a full monthly retirement benefit for a period and is approved for disability benefits; Social Security will make up the difference between the early retirement amount and the full disability amount for those months the individual was disabled but receiving early retirement benefits (retroactively).

Example 5-1

Tracy Roberts quit work at 62 (clearly younger than his full retirement age) due to health problems. He received early retirement benefits for a time, then obtained approval for disability benefits. If Social Security agreed that Tracy's disability commenced before he started to collect early retirement benefits, it would pay him the difference between his disability payment (at his age would be equal to his full retirement payment) and his early retirement payment for those months during which he received early retirement payments. (Recall that the difference between the early retirement benefit at age 62 and the disability payment after 62 is currently 25% of full PIA.) In other words, when Tracy reaches his full retirement age, he would receive his PIA benefit, as if he had never elected to collect early retirement payments.

Disability benefit eligibility

The number of Social Security credits or quarters that a disabled applicant needs to qualify for disability benefits depends on the age at which the applicant becomes disabled. Generally, an applicant needs 40 credits, 20 of which were earned in the last 10 years ending with the year in which the disability started. Keep in mind, that unlike retirement benefits in which 40 quarters establishes a fully insured status going forward, for SSDI benefits, the covered quarters needed to have occurred immediately before the disability began.

However, younger workers may qualify with fewer credits. The rules are as follows:

- *Before age 24*—A disabled applicant may qualify having earned six credits in the three-year period ending when the disability begins.
- *Age 24 to 31*—A disabled applicant may qualify having credits attributable to working half the time between age 21 and when the disability commences.
  - For example, if Tiffany became disabled at age 27, she would need to have FICA credits or quarters for three working years (12 credits) out of the past six years (between her ages 21 and 27).
- *Age 31 or older*—In general, the disabled applicant must have earned the number of work credits shown in the chart that follows.

Unless the applicant is blind, he or she must have earned at least 20 of the credits in the 10 years immediately preceding the onset of disability.

Born after 1929, became disabled at age	Number of credits needed
31 through 42	20
44	22
46	24
48	26
50	28
52	30
54	32
56	34
58	36
60	38
62 or older	40

Source: SSA

For example, if Sylva was born in 1980 and became disabled at age 48, she would need 26 credits or quarters to be eligible for Social Security disability benefits.

Unique rules for blind applicants

There are special rules for people who are blind or who suffer from very low vision. The SSA considers an applicant for SSDI benefits to be legally blind under Social Security rules if that individual's vision cannot be corrected to better than 20/20 in the better eye, or if the individual's visual field is 20 degrees or less, even with a corrective lens. Certain applicants who qualify for disability benefits may still have some sight and may be able to read large print and ambulate without a cane or a guide dog.

If an applicant does not satisfy the SSA's definition of blindness, he or she may still qualify for disability benefits if vision problems alone or combined with other health problems impair the individual's ability to earn income from working.

There are a number of special rules for people who are blind that recognize the severe impact of blindness on a person's ability to work. For example, the monthly earnings limit for people who are blind is generally higher than the limit that applies to nonblind disabled workers. In 2019, the monthly earnings limit for a blind disability income benefit claimant to still be considered disabled is $2,040.

Obtaining benefits

Unlike retirement benefits, one cannot complete the application process for SSDI benefits entirely online (although certain documents may be submitted online). Typically, the applicant or a representative of the applicant must make an appointment to appear at a local Social Security office.

Compassionate allowances

Social Security has developed a list of more than 225 compassionate allowances currently, which, if the insured person has one of these conditions, shortens the time frame for being approved for disability benefits to approximately two weeks.

The allowances can be found at http://ssa.gov/compassionateallowances/conditions.htm

Region 1: Boston Social Security Disability

- Connecticut Social Security Disability
- Maine Social Security Disability
- Massachusetts Social Security Disability
- New Hampshire Social Security Disability
- Rhode Island Social Security Disability
- Vermont Social Security Disability

Region 2: New York Social Security Disability

- New Jersey Social Security Disability
- New York Social Security Disability
- Puerto Rico Social Security Disability
- U.S. Virgin Islands Social Security Disability

Region 3: Philadelphia Social Security Disability

- Delaware Social Security Disability
- Maryland Social Security Disability
- Pennsylvania Social Security Disability
- Virginia Social Security Disability
- West Virginia Social Security Disability
- District of Columbia Social Security Disability

Region 4: Atlanta Social Security Disability

- Alabama Social Security Disability
- Florida Social Security Disability
- Georgia Social Security Disability

- Kentucky Social Security Disability
- Mississippi Social Security Disability
- North Carolina Social Security Disability
- South Carolina Social Security Disability
- Tennessee Social Security Disability

Region 5: Chicago Social Security Disability

- Illinois Social Security Disability
- Indiana Social Security Disability
- Michigan Social Security Disability
- Minnesota Social Security Disability
- Ohio Social Security Disability
- Wisconsin Social Security Disability

Region 6: Dallas Social Security Disability

- Arkansas Social Security Disability
- Louisiana Social Security Disability
- New Mexico Social Security Disability
- Oklahoma Social Security Disability
- Texas Social Security Disability

Region 7: Kansas City Social Security Disability

- Iowa Social Security Disability
- Nebraska Social Security Disability
- Kansas Social Security Disability
- Missouri Social Security Disability

Region 8: Denver Social Security Disability

- Colorado Social Security Disability
- Montana Social Security Disability
- North Dakota Social Security Disability
- South Dakota Social Security Disability
- Utah Social Security Disability
- Wyoming Social Security Disability

Region 9: San Francisco Social Security Disability

- Arizona Social Security Disability
- California Social Security Disability
- Hawaii Social Security Disability
- Nevada Social Security Disability
- American Samoa, Guam, and Northern Marina Islands Social Security Disability

Region 10: Seattle Social Security Disability

- Alaska Social Security Disability
- Idaho Social Security Disability

- Oregon Social Security Disability
- Washington Social Security Disability

If someone suffered a disabling injury in January and met Social Security's disability definition, he or she would become eligible for the first disability payment for July. The average SSDI payment in July of 2018 is $1,199. The maximum disability benefit in 2019 is $2,861.

Denial of claims

If an individual's application for SSD is denied (we can see from the following table that most initial applications are), he or she can appeal the decision. A denied applicant must request a review of the denial within 60 days from the date of the denial letter. The first step of the appeal process in most states is the request for reconsideration, a review of the claimant's file by another claims examiner. If the applicant is denied again, he or she may appeal to the next level by requesting a hearing with an administrative law judge who works for the SSA.

The SSA recently met its goal to increase the number of administrative law judges to more than 1,500. With more than 255,000 hearing requests in 2017, individuals should consider legal representation when preparing for their disability appeals.

Selected data from Social Security's disability program

The following table presents unedited data (including corrections, if any) on disabled worker beneficiaries paid from Social Security's Disability Insurance Trust Fund. In particular, unedited award data may contain duplicate cases.

	Disabled worker beneficiary statistics by calendar year, quarter, and month											
	Number of applications		Awards					In current payment status		Terminations[e]		
					Ratio to applications[d]							
Time period	Field office receipts[a]	Initial DDS receipts[b]	Number[c]	Increase over prior period	Field office receipts	Initial DDS receipts	Number at end of period	Increase over prior period	Number	Increase over prior period	Termi-nation rate
				—By Calendar Year—								
2004	2,137,531	1,561,059	797,226	2.48%	37.30%	51.07%	6,201,362	5.58%	466,332	3.46%	7.32%
2005	2,122,109	1,482,475	832,201	4.39%	39.22%	56.14%	6,524,582	5.21%	494,592	6.06%	7.36%
2006	2,134,088	1,471,122	812,596	-2.36%	38.08%	55.24%	6,811,679	4.40%	513,292	3.78%	7.28%
2007	2,190,196	1,470,748	823,106	1.29%	37.58%	55.97%	7,101,355	4.25%	525,012	2.28%	7.14%
2008	2,320,396	1,527,108	895,011	8.74%	38.57%	58.61%	7,427,203	4.59%	564,518	7.52%	7.34%
2009	2,816,244	1,798,975	985,940	10.16%	35.01%	54.81%	7,789,113	4.87%	628,478	11.33%	7.79%
2010	2,935,798	1,926,398	1,052,551	6.76%	35.85%	54.64%	8,204,710	5.34%	646,387	2.85%	7.64%
2011	2,878,920	1,859,591	1,025,003	-2.62%	35.60%	55.12%	8,576,067	4.53%	656,902	1.63%	7.42%

| | Number of applications | | Awards | | | | In current payment status | | Terminations[e] | | |
| | | | | | Ratio to applications[d] | | | | | | |
Time period	Field office receipts[a]	Initial DDS receipts[b]	Number[c]	Increase over prior period	Field office receipts	Initial DDS receipts	Number at end of period	Increase over prior period	Number	Increase over prior period	Termination rate
2012	2,824,024	1,808,863	979,973	-4.39%	34.70%	54.18%	8,827,795	2.94%	726,432	10.58%	7.90%
2013	2,653,939	1,702,700	884,894	-9.70%	33.34%	51.97%	8,942,584	1.30%	767,738	5.69%	8.17%
2014	2,536,174	1,633,652	810,973	-8.35%	31.98%	49.64%	8,954,518	0.13%	793,646	3.37%	8.37%
2015	2,427,443	1,552,119	775,739	-4.34%	31.96%	49.98%	8,909,430	-0.50%	817,045	2.95%	8.62%
2016	2,321,583	1,473,700	744,268	-4.06%	32.06%	50.50%	8,808,736	-1.13%	830,044	1.59%	8.81%
2017	2,179,928	1,377,803	762,141	2.40%	34.96%	55.32%	8,695,475	-1.29%	868,795	4.67%	9.30%
2018	2,073,293	1,300,668	733,879	-3.71%	35.40%	56.42%	8,537,332	-1.82%	888,214	2.24%	9.63%
—By Quarter—											
2015 Q2	638,754	414,104	206,392	9.83%	32.31%	49.84%	8,937,961	0.03%	202,486	-1.88%	2.21%
2015 Q3	614,438	392,361	194,443	-5.79%	31.65%	49.56%	8,921,350	-0.19%	209,710	3.57%	2.29%
2015 Q4	565,932	360,956	186,983	-3.84%	33.04%	51.80%	8,909,430	-0.13%	198,493	-5.35%	2.17%
2016 Q1	578,655	363,223	185,123	-0.99%	31.99%	50.97%	8,888,588	-0.23%	203,524	2.53%	2.23%
2016 Q2	598,009	379,566	196,205	5.99%	32.81%	51.69%	8,872,165	-0.18%	206,988	1.70%	2.27%
2016 Q3	627,794	400,933	190,045	-3.14%	30.27%	47.40%	8,841,345	-0.35%	216,542	4.62%	2.38%
2016 Q4	517,125	329,978	172,895	-9.02%	33.43%	52.40%	8,808,736	-0.37%	202,990	-6.26%	2.24%
2017 Q1	561,965	352,802	193,674	12.02%	34.46%	54.90%	8,778,443	-0.34%	221,796	9.26%	2.45%
2017 Q2	562,813	356,315	196,430	1.42%	34.90%	55.13%	8,755,405	-0.26%	214,630	-3.23%	2.38%
2017 Q3	548,088	341,902	201,820	2.74%	36.82%	59.03%	8,736,086	-0.22%	222,406	3.62%	2.47%
2017 Q4	507,062	326,784	170,217	-15.66%	33.57%	52.09%	8,695,475	-0.46%	209,963	-5.59%	2.34%
2018 Q1	538,077	327,935	188,681	10.85%	35.07%	57.54%	8,653,039	-0.49%	228,986	9.06%	2.56%
2018 Q2	549,790	342,870	189,439	0.40%	34.46%	55.25%	8,622,658	-0.35%	215,663	-5.82%	2.42%
2018 Q3	548,872	335,906	190,492	0.56%	34.71%	56.71%	8,585,452	-0.43%	229,348	6.35%	2.58%
2018 Q4	436,554	293,957	165,267	-13.24%	37.86%	56.22%	8,537,332	-0.56%	214,217	-6.60%	2.42%
2019 Q1	501,029	318,441	193,127	16.86%	38.55%	60.65%	8,504,781	-0.38%	226,238	5.61%	2.57%

Disabled worker beneficiary statistics by calendar year, quarter, and month (continued)

Disabled worker beneficiary statistics by calendar year, quarter, and month (continued)											

Time period	Number of applications		Awards				In current payment status		Terminations[e]		
	Field office receipts[a]	Initial DDS receipts[b]	Numberc	Increase over prior period	Ratio to applications[d]		Number at end of period	Increase over prior period	Number	Increase over prior period	Termi-nation rate
					Field office receipts	Initial DDS receipts					
					—By Month—						
2018 Jan	156,670	91,564	67,036	16.51%	42.79%	73.21%	8,677,460	-0.21%	82,688	15.93%	0.93%
2018 Feb	169,070	104,115	51,934	-22.53%	30.72%	49.88%	8,663,192	-0.16%	67,621	-18.22%	0.76%
2018 Mar	212,337	132,256	69,711	34.23%	32.83%	52.71%	8,653,039	-0.12%	78,677	16.35%	0.89%
2018 Apr	172,088	108,698	65,387	-6.20%	38.00%	60.15%	8,645,567	-0.09%	71,700	-8.87%	0.81%
2018 May	170,296	107,301	59,876	-8.43%	35.16%	55.80%	8,633,765	-0.14%	69,550	-3.00%	0.79%
2018 Jun	207,406	126,871	64,176	7.18%	30.94%	50.58%	8,622,658	-0.13%	74,413	6.99%	0.84%
2018 Jul	164,037	100,311	66,154	3.08%	40.33%	65.95%	8,611,522	-0.13%	77,677	4.39%	0.88%
2018 Aug	219,272	135,213	60,048	-9.23%	27.39%	44.41%	8,596,559	-0.17%	75,852	-2.35%	0.86%
2018 Sep	165,563	100,382	64,290	7.06%	38.83%	64.05%	8,585,452	-0.13%	75,819	-0.04%	0.86%
2018 Oct	143,689	101,512	63,366	-1.44%	44.10%	62.42%	8,573,763	-0.14%	76,413	0.78%	0.87%
2018 Nov	169,792	111,839	47,715	-24.70%	28.10%	42.66%	8,557,051	-0.19%	65,266	-14.59%	0.74%
2018 Dec	123,073	80,606	54,186	13.56%	44.03%	67.22%	8,537,332	-0.23%	72,538	11.14%	0.83%
2019 Jan	144,192	90,450	65,077	20.10%	45.13%	71.95%	8,520,503	-0.20%	81,602	12.50%	0.93%
2019 Feb	151,863	95,912	58,088	-10.74%	38.25%	60.56%	8,510,897	-0.11%	69,098	-15.32%	0.79%
2019 Mar	204,974	132,079	69,962	20.44%	34.13%	52.97%	8,504,781	-0.07%	75,538	9.32%	0.87%

[a]The number of applications is for disabled-worker benefits only and, as such, excludes disabled child's and disabled widow(er)'s benefits. These applications are those received at Social Security field offices, teleservice centers, and claims filed electronically on the internet. Applications ultimately result in either a denial or award of benefits. These counts include applications that are denied because the individual is not insured for disability benefits.

Because the application data are tabulated on a weekly basis, some months include 5 weeks of data while others include only 4 weeks. This weekly method of tabulation accounts for much of the month-to-month variation in the monthly application data. This method also occasionally causes quarterly data to have either 12 or 14 weeks of data instead of 13 weeks, annual data may include an extra week of data.

[b]Receipts at State Disability Determination Services (DDS), Federal Disability Units, Disability Processing Branches, and Extended Service Team Sites for an initial evaluation of whether the claimant's disability meets the definition of disability as set forth in the Social Security Act and appropriate regulations.

[c]Award data prior to 2014 are unedited and may contain duplicates.

[d]Awards as a ratio to applications is a crude measure and does not represent an allowance rate. This ratio expresses the number of awards in a given time period as a ratio to the number of applications in the same time period. Some of the awards in any time period, however, resulted from applications in previous time period(s).

[e]The number of terminations is the number of beneficiaries who leave the disability rolls for any reason. The number is calculated on the basis of the change in the total number of entitled beneficiaries (those in current payment status plus those whose benefits are withheld for any reason) and the number of awards. The termination rate is the ratio of the terminations to the number of beneficiaries who could potentially leave the rolls. This latter number is approximated as the sum of the number entitled at the beginning of the time period plus half the number of awards in that period.

Reducing benefits due to payments by other government type disability payments

If someone is entitled to receive disability benefits from private long-term disability insurance benefits, these benefits will have no impact on the insured's SSDI benefits. However, if someone is claiming SSDI benefits and simultaneously receives government-regulated disability benefits, such as workers' comp benefits or temporary state disability benefits, they can end up reducing SSDI benefits. The rule is that a disabled SSDI recipient may not receive more than 80% of the average amount earned before the disability ensued in combined SSDI and other disability benefits. If that occurs, the SSDI benefit will be reduced. SSI and Veterans Benefits Administration (VA) benefits (not disability benefits) will not reduce an individual's SSDI benefit.

No disability payments at full retirement age and older

If one is still receiving disability insurance by the time of his or her full retirement age, the payments morph into retirement benefits. The amount of the retirement payments remains the same.

Back pay for delayed benefit approval

Because initial denial of claims for SSDI occur in roughly 60% of situations, when approval finally happens, retroactive benefits—back pay—is not uncommon. The amount available in back pay, of course, depends on the applicant's SSDI monthly amount. The number of months of back payments one gets will be determined by the months between the application date and the established date of onset (when the applicant's disability started). If an individual previously applied for disability benefits, he or she may be able to get back pay going back to the original application date.

Waiting or elimination period

Disability benefit payments start only after the applicant has been disabled for five months, then continue until the benefit recipient's condition has improved to the level that he or she is able to return to work.

Knowledge check

1. What is the waiting period for SSDI benefits?

    a. 3 months.
    b. 5 months.
    c. 9 months.
    d. 24 months.

Generally no benefit for disabled children

Generally, children cannot qualify for SSDI because such benefits are available only to disabled workers having sufficient FICA credits or quarters. (However, if a disabled child's parent is eligible for Social Security retirement or disability, the child may be able to receive a dependent's benefit called the disabled adult child benefit after turning 18.)

If a worker's adult child is disabled before the age of 22, he or she can qualify for benefits based on a parent's earnings record. Anyone who becomes disabled after turning 22 needs to pass the recent work test, a measure of how many years of work the disabled individual has performed depending on his or her age.

The Medicare or Medicaid piece

After collecting disability benefits for 24 months, a beneficiary will become eligible for Medicare, regardless of that beneficiary's age. In the interim, if the disabled individual's income and assets fall less than certain benchmarks, that person may qualify for Medicaid benefits.

Medical eligibility for Social Security disability income benefits

An applicant must suffer from a medical condition that meets the SSA's definition of disability. SSDI benefits are eligible only to those with a severe, long-term, total disability. Severe means that the condition must interfere with work-related tasks. *Long term* means that the claimant's condition has lasted or is expected to last at least one year.

A crucial part of claiming benefits under either Social Security program is proving that one is severely disabled—essentially that the claimant has a physical or mental condition that prevents him or her from doing any substantial gainful activity (SGA) and will last at least one year or will cause that individual's death.

The fact that one's doctor may have advised someone not to work, or that he or she feels too ill to work, does not necessarily mean that the SSA will consider that individual to be disabled.

The SSA evaluates disability using its own medical experts, based on a list of physical and mental conditions contained in its regulations.

Furthermore, the impairment or combination of impairments must be of such severity that the applicant is not only unable to do his or her previous work but cannot, considering his or her age, education, and work experience, engage in any other kind of substantial gainful work which exists in the national economy.

Defining total disability

Total disability means the inability to perform SGA for at least one year. If a claimant is currently working and makes more than $1,220 per month in 2019, ($2,040 for blind applicants), the SSA will deem that individual to be performing SGA and not disabled enough to qualify for SSDI benefits.

Can one have earnings and still collect benefits?

Monthly substantial gainful activity amounts by disability type								
Year	Blind	Non-blind	Year	Blind	Non-blind	Year	Blind	Non-blind
1975	$200	$200	1990	$780	$500	2005	$1,380	$ 830
1976	230	230	1991	810	500	2006	1,450	860
1977	240	240	1992	850	500	2007	1,500	900
1978	334	260	1993	880	500	2008	1,570	940

Year	Blind	Non-blind	Year	Blind	Non-blind	Year	Blind	Non-blind
1979	375	280	1994	930	500	2009	1,640	980
1980	417	300	1995	940	500	2010	1,640	1,000
1981	459	300	1996	960	500	2011	1,640	1,000
1982	500	300	1997	1,000	500	2012	1,690	1,010
1983	550	300	1998	1,050	500	2013	1,740	1,040
1984	580	300	1999	1,110	700[a]	2014	1,800	1,070
1985	610	300	2000	1,170	700	2015	1,820	1,090
1986	650	300	2001	1,240	740	2016	1,820	1,130
1987	680	300	2002	1,300	780	2017	1,950	1,170
1988	700	300	2003	1,330	800	2018	1,980	1,180
1989	740	300	2004	1,350	810	2019	2,040	1,220

Monthly substantial gainful activity amounts by disability type (continued)

[a] $500 amount applied in the first half of 1999.

In some cases, earnings can be reduced by the costs associated with work, such as paying for a wheelchair or services of an attendant. If an individual qualifies for disability benefits, he or she will not receive SSDI benefits until that individual has satisfied a five-month waiting (elimination) period. If the disabled beneficiary's application is approved, the first Social Security benefit will be paid for the sixth full month after the date when the SSA deems the beneficiary's disability to have begun.

In July 2018, the average monthly SSDI benefit was $1,199.

In reality, it is a six-month wait. Social Security benefits are paid in the month following the month for which they are due. In other words, the benefit due for December would be paid in January of the following year, and so on.

Example 5-2

Shirley Schneider's disability from muscular dystrophy began on June 15, 2019, and she was immediately approved for benefits. Shirley's first benefit would be paid for the month of December 2019, the sixth (not the fifth) full month of disability.

Knowledge check

2. Unless an applicant is relatively young, what is the general eligibility requirement for Social Security disability income benefits?

   a. Forty credits, 20 of which were earned in the last 10 years ending with the year in which the disability started.
   b. Six credits in the three-year period ending with the year in which the disability started.
   c. Three working years (12 credits) out of the past six years, ending with the year in which the disability started.
   d. 20–40 work credits.

Back (retroactive) pay

Even if the applicant is approved immediately (for example, because he or she recently had a lung transplant), that individual would have to wait. Typically, an applicant is not approved for six months to a year (after at least one level of appeal). In that situation, when the claim is finally approved, that claimant would be paid disability back pay starting with the sixth month after the disability began (the disability onset date).

After an applicant is paid any outstanding back pay, a monthly disability benefit follows. That benefit may or may not be taxable. A disabled claimant's family members may also be eligible for a monthly benefit that is generally less than the benefit paid to the eligible disabled worker.

Please see the chapter on Taxation of Social Security Benefits for a discussion on the taxation of back pay.

Working while collecting disability benefits

Trial work period—The trial work period allows a patient to test his or her ability to work for at least nine months. During the trial work period, the patient will receive full Social Security benefits regardless of how much is being earned as long as he or she reports the work and continues to have a disability. In 2019, a trial work month is any month during which total earnings are more than $880. If the patient is self-employed, he or she has a trial work month when he or she can earn more than $880 (after expenses) or work more than 80 hours in his or her own business. The trial work period continues until the patient has worked nine months within a 60-month period.

Extended period of eligibility—After the trial work period, the patient has 36 months during which he or she can work and still receive benefits for any month that earnings aren't substantial. During a trial work period, neither a new application nor disability decision is necessary to get the Social Security disability benefit.

Expedited reinstatement—If benefits stop because of substantial earnings, the patient has five years to ask the SSA to restart the benefits if the patient is unable to keep working because of the condition. The patient won't have to file a new application or wait for benefits to restart while the medical condition is being reviewed.

Continuation of Medicare—If Social Security disability benefits stop because of earnings, but the patient is still disabled, free Medicare Part A coverage will continue for at least 93 months after the 9-month trial work period.

Continuing disability review

The SSA is required by law to periodically review the case of every person who is receiving Social Security Disability (SSD) or SSI disability benefits. This process is called a continuing disability review (CDR). Its purpose is to identify beneficiaries who may no longer qualify as disabled. If, during a CDR, the SSA finds that a claimant's medical condition has improved enough so that he or she can work, that individual's Social Security benefits will end.

In general, it is much easier for a disabled individual to pass a CDR than it is to be granted benefits initially.

The frequency at which CDRs occur will vary.

CDRs for adults

Most claims are set for review every three or seven years, depending on the likelihood that a benefit recipient's condition will improve. If a claimant has a condition that is expected to medically improve, a CDR may be conducted even sooner than three years. In contrast, Social Security beneficiaries whose condition is not expected to improve or are disabled due to a permanent condition (such as a lost limb or impaired intellectual functioning) may have their claim reviewed even less than every seven years.

However, even those with permanent disability conditions may be eventually subject to CDRs. Further, CDRs are also more frequently conducted for beneficiaries who are age 50.

CDRs for children receiving disability benefits under SSI

Children who are receiving (needs based, not regular Social Security) SSI disability benefits will automatically have their claims reviewed when they turn 18. The standards that must be met for an adult to be considered disabled are different from those for a child. Therefore, at age 18, the child will be evaluated under the adult standards. Newborns who receive SSI due to a low-birth weight will have their claim reviewed prior to the one-year mark.

Knowledge check

3. According to the SSA, what does total disability mean?

    a. The inability of the insured to perform any substantial gainful activity for at least one year.
    b. The inability of the insured to perform the tasks associated with the job at which he or she was employed when the disability began.
    c. The inability to stand or sit for extended periods.
    d. That one's doctor has advised someone not to work.

Triggered continued disability reviews

In addition to the regularly scheduled CDRs, the SSA may conduct a CDR in any of the following situations:

- The benefit recipient returned to work.
- The benefit recipient informed the SSA of an improvement in condition.
- Medical evidence indicates that the benefit recipient's condition has improved.
- A third party informs the SSA that the benefit recipient is not following treatment protocol.
- A new treatment for the benefit recipient's disabling condition has recently been introduced.

Continuing disability review process

If a disability income benefit recipient's Social Security claim is up for review, the SSA will notify that individual by mail. The SSA will send either a copy of the short form, Disability Update Report (SSA-455-OCR-SM) or the long form, Continuing Disability Review Report (SSA-454-BK), announcing a CDR. The short form is generally for those whose condition is not expected to improve, and is only two pages long.

If a benefit recipient's condition could improve, or if his or her answers on the short form concern the SSA, the agency will respond by sending the benefit recipient the long form. The long form is similar to the initial disability application at 10 pages long. The form will question whether the benefit recipient saw a doctor, was hospitalized in the past year, whether the recipient underwent medical tests in the past year, such as electrocardiograms, blood tests, or x-rays, and, whether that disability income benefit recipient was working.

A benefit recipient is encouraged to submit any updated medical evidence to the SSA, although the SSA may also obtain such information on their own. In general, the SSA will be reviewing the period of 12 months prior to the notice, although the agency can examine evidence from any time after a recipient was initially granted benefits.

Medical improvement review standard

Assuming that an SSDI benefit recipient has not returned to work, the SSA will first determine whether there has been medical improvement in that claimant's condition. If improvement is not substantiated then the CDR process is complete, and the disabled individual's benefits (and auxiliary benefits) will not be affected.

In contrast, if the answer is yes, the SSA will then decide if the medical improvement affects the benefit recipient's ability (or inability) to work. Assuming it does not, the disability benefits would continue. But if the SSA comes to the conclusion that the benefit recipient's condition has improved to the point where he or she can return to work, that person will be notified that benefit payments will stop and will be given the chance to appeal the decision.

If the SSA feels that the evidence is insufficient to decide, or if there are inconsistencies between what the benefit recipient reports and medical evidence, the benefit recipient may be required to participate in for a consultative examination, which is an examination by a doctor that is paid for by Social Security.

Timelines for requesting continued benefits

Certain deadlines for requesting that disability benefits continue apply to both SSDI and SSI.

A request for reconsideration must be filed within 60 days after receiving a notice of determination.

Users generally have three options when requesting reconsideration, as follows:

1. Case review—An independent review of the record with or without additional evidence. This is the only option available in cases involving the medical aspects of a disability denial of an initial application.
2. Informal conference—A review as in (1) in which users may participate. Users may present witnesses and may present the case in person.
3. Formal conference—Same as (2), and user may request that adverse witnesses be issued a subpoena and cross-examined by the user or a representative. This type of reconsideration applies only in adverse post-eligibility situations (that is, when SSI payments are going to be reduced, suspended, or terminated).

Request for reconsideration

If benefits were stopped because of medical improvement, the individual who claims to continue to meet Social Security's definition of disability can request a face-to-face hearing with a disability-hearing officer, even at the reconsideration stage.

Request for hearing

If the claimant's request for reconsideration is denied, the claimant must file a request for hearing, and a request for continuing benefits, within 10 days after receiving the notice of adverse action. One may elect continuing benefits along with a hearing request even if he or she did not elect continuing benefits when filing the initial request for reconsideration. To continue receiving benefits, one must file a request for reconsideration (appeal) within 10 days of receiving the notice of cessation along with a request for continuing cash benefits, Medicare, or both. Note that this time limit is much shorter than the 60 days for the appeal itself.

If the claimant files the request for continuing benefits later than 10 days after receiving the notice of cessation or reconsideration, Social Security will deny the request for continuing benefits, unless the person making the request can show good cause for the late filing.

Further appeals

If one's appeal is denied at the hearing level and that individual still wishes to appeal to the Appeals Council, he or she will no longer continue to receive disability benefits. However, if the Appeals Council remands the appellee's case for a new hearing, benefits will continue with no action on the appellee's part. One can also choose to continue benefits for others (such as children) receiving benefits based on the covered worker's earnings record.

Completing the benefit election request form

The benefit election request form, Form SSA-795, *Statement of Claimant or Other Person*, can be downloaded from the Social Security website (SSA.gov). The form has a simple checkbox format, but an accompanying letter should also explain briefly, but specifically, why benefits should continue.

Continuing disability benefits for others

When a claimant requests to have one's own benefits continued while appealing the cessation of his or her benefits, that appealing party should also request to continue benefits for others that were based on the appellee's earnings record. However, the other persons receiving benefits based upon the appellee's earnings record must also make their *own* election to receive continuing benefits: Each beneficiary must also make his or her own election to receive continuing benefits during the appeal period.

After the appellee requests continuing benefits for others receiving benefits on his or her earnings record, Social Security will advise those people of their right to elect to receive continuing benefits, and they then can respond with their own elections to receive (or not receive) continuing benefits.

Continuing SSI and Medicaid benefits

If one elects continuing SSI benefits and was eligible for Medicaid before receiving a cessation notice, Medicaid benefits will continue automatically. One's needs-based SSI benefits may be suspended or changed while his or her appeal is pending if the appellee's living circumstances change (typically changes in income, excess resources, or different living arrangements).

Working while appealing

If an individual received SSDI and worked at what would be considered substantially gainful employment during a trial work period while waiting for an appeal, that person's SSDI benefits may be suspended.

When SSDI benefits will end

The general rule is that a claimant is no longer considered as disabled for purposes of receiving SSDI benefits in the month in which the cessation notice is mailed to the benefit recipient. Presuming that the recipient does not request a continuation of benefits, then his or her SSDI or SSI benefits will continue during the disability cessation month and the following two months (the grace period).

For example, on July 15, Carolyn received an SSDI cessation notice. She has responded well to a new drug and has experienced meaningful medical improvement. The last month for which she is able for the disability month is September unless she elects continuing benefits within 10 days after receiving the notice of cessation (and that the SSA receives it within 15 days).

Keep in mind that a claimant's disability benefits might be suspended for specified reasons during the CDR process, such as failure to cooperate with Social Security by refusing a medical exam, the inability of Social Security to establish the claimant's whereabouts, or unjustified failure to follow prescribed treatment. Even in these cases, the claimant has the same 10-day period from the receipt of the notice of cessation to elect continuing benefits.

Knowledge check

4. Helen is currently receiving Social Security disability income benefits. However, there is a real possibility that her condition may improve. In typical circumstances, how frequently will Social Security review whether her disability benefits should continue?

    a. Five months.
    b. Annually.
    c. Every three years or fewer.
    d. Every seven years or more.

Example 5-3

Crawford Lockhart was issued an SSDI cessation notice on July 15 because he failed to attend, without good cause, a medical exam scheduled by Social Security on May 15. The situation is treated as if Crawford's disability ended in May. His benefits will continue only until the end of July. However, Crawford does have 10 days after receipt of his notice to elect continuing benefits.

Repayment of denied benefits

If appeal is unsuccessful at any level, Social Security will ask the individual whose claim has been denied to repay the SSDI or SSI cash benefits that were paid while the appeal was pending. Social Security will not require repayment of the value of any Medicare or Medicaid benefits that continued while the appeal was pending.

Waiver opportunity

Social Security will consider waiving the recovery of disability benefits paid while an appeal is pending as long as the person who had received the benefits before the denial had appealed the cessation of benefits in good faith. An appeal is presumed to be made in good faith unless the individual filing the appeal failed to cooperate with Social Security during the appeal. Not cooperating generally means failing without good reason to provide medical or other information requested by Social Security or failing without good reason to attend a physical or mental examination.

Example 5-4

During Minnie's appeal for SSDI benefits (which was ultimately denied), she received provisional benefits. She may be granted a waiver from having to repay them if she cooperated during the appeal process by providing medical records and agreeing to be examined by the medical professionals who were assigned to her case.

When determining whether an individual had good cause for failure to cooperate, Social Security will consider any physical, mental, educational or linguistic limitations (such as inability to speak or read English) that may have contributed to that individual's failure to cooperate.

Supplemental Security Income

SSI is a federal program that pays monthly benefits to low-income aged, blind, and disabled individuals. The SSA runs the program, which is financed from general tax revenues, rather than from Social Security (FICA) taxes. The SSI definition of disability for adult applicants is the same as the test in the SSDI program. Only individuals having low incomes and limited financial assets are eligible for SSI. Women comprise the majority of adults receiving SSI.

Although the SSI program is run by the SSA, operationally, it is actually a cooperative program between the SSA and the applicant's state's government. In that light, one's eligibility, as well as the amount of benefits receivable, ultimately depend on the applicant's state of residence. For federal SSI purposes (and most states reasonably follow these guidelines), one must meet all the following three criteria:

- Be blind, disabled, or age 65 or over
- Be either a citizen of the United States, or meet very narrow requirements based on U.S. permanent residency, military service, or political asylum or refugee status
- Have a low income
  - Only about half of the beneficiary's actual income will be considered, but this counted income cannot be higher than an amount set by the applicant's state of residence, typically from $700 to $1,400 per month. However, some states allow people with higher incomes to receive state benefits.
  - The assets owned (minus certain items, such one auto and the home) must be worth less than $2,000, ($3,000 for a couple).

If the application is approved, SSI benefits will include cash payments at a minimum of $771 per month for an individual or $1,157 per month for a couple (2019). The applicant's state of residence may supplement this amount with an additional payment (the State Supplementary Payment). Any federally provided SSI benefits have been adjusted for annual inflation.

SSI and old-age, survivors, and disability insurance (OASDI) program rates and limits

See appendix A for 2019 rates and limits and appendix B for 2018 rates and limits

This data can be found at: https://www.ssa.gov/policy/docs/quickfacts/prog_highlights/index.html.

Knowledge check

5. In March of the current year, the SSA notified George that he is no longer eligible for Social Security disability income benefits. Presuming that George does not appeal the decision, for how long, if at all, would his benefits continue?

    a. He would receive a check for March and benefits would stop immediately after.
    b. He would receive checks for March and April.
    c. He would receive checks for March, April, and May.
    d. He would receive checks for March and through the following six months.

Summary

We learned the importance of SSDI for many Americans. We examined how work history affects benefit eligibility, as well as the amount of the benefit itself. Social Security's stringent definition of disability is arguably harsh. Its process for reviewing claims from a medical perspective operates at several levels. Because most initial claims for Social Security disability benefits are denied, it is important to understand the appeal process and how benefits may be paid during the appeal or that back pay can be the result of the delay and ultimate approval. Briefly, we covered how SSI operates as a needs-based program distinct from traditional Social Security.

Appendix A

OASDI AND SSI PROGRAM RATES & LIMITS 2019

Old-Age, Survivors, and Disability Insurance (OASDI)

Tax Rates (percent)
Social Security (Old-Age, Survivors, and Disability Insurance)
Employers and Employees, each [a]	6.20

Medicare (Hospital Insurance)
Employers and Employees, each [a,b]	1.45

Maximum Taxable Earnings (dollars)
Social Security	132,900
Medicare (Hospital Insurance)	No limit

Earnings Required for Work Credits (dollars)
One Work Credit (One Quarter of Coverage)	1,360
Maximum of Four Credits a Year	5,440

Earnings Test Annual Exempt Amount (dollars)
Under Full Retirement Age for Entire Year	17,640
For Months Before Reaching Full Retirement Age in Given Year	46,920
Beginning with Month Reaching Full Retirement Age	No limit

Maximum Monthly Social Security Benefit for
Workers Retiring at Full Retirement Age (dollars)	2,861

Full Retirement Age	66

Cost-of-Living Adjustment (percent)	2.8

a. Self-employed persons pay a total of 15.3 percent—12.4 percent for OASDI and 2.9 percent for Medicare.
b. This rate does not reflect the additional 0.9 percent in Medicare taxes certain high-income taxpayers are required to pay. See IRS information on this topic.

Supplemental Security Income (SSI)

Monthly Federal Payment Standard (dollars)
Individual	771
Couple	1,157

Cost-of-Living Adjustment (percent)	2.8

Resource Limits (dollars)
Individual	2,000
Couple	3,000

Monthly Income Exclusions (dollars)
Earned Income [a]	65
Unearned Income	20

Substantial Gainful Activity (SGA) Level for the Nonblind Disabled (dollars)	1,220

a. The earned income exclusion consists of the first $65 of monthly earnings, plus one-half of remaining earnings.

Office of Retirement and Disability Policy
www.ssa.gov/policy

Produced and published at U.S. taxpayer expense

Appendix B

OASDI AND SSI PROGRAM RATES & LIMITS 2018

OASDI and SSI Program Rates & Limits 2018

Old-Age, Survivors, and Disability Insurance (OASDI)

Tax Rates (percent)
Social Security (Old-Age, Survivors, and Disability Insurance)
Employers and Employees, each [a] ... 6.20
Medicare (Hospital Insurance)
Employers and Employees, each [a,b] ... 1.45

Maximum Taxable Earnings (dollars)
Social Security ... 128,400
Medicare (Hospital Insurance) ... No limit

Earnings Required for Work Credits (dollars)
One Work Credit (One Quarter of Coverage) ... 1,320
Maximum of Four Credits a Year ... 5,280

Earnings Test Annual Exempt Amount (dollars)
Under Full Retirement Age for Entire Year ... 17,040
For Months Before Reaching Full Retirement Age in Given Year ... 45,360
Beginning with Month Reaching Full Retirement Age ... No limit

Maximum Monthly Social Security Benefit for
Workers Retiring at Full Retirement Age (dollars) ... 2,788

Full Retirement Age ... 66

Cost-of-Living Adjustment (percent) ... 2.0

a. Self-employed persons pay a total of 15.3 percent—12.4 percent for OASDI and 2.9 percent for Medicare.
b. This rate does not reflect the additional 0.9 percent in Medicare taxes certain high-income taxpayers are required to pay. See IRS information on this topic.

Supplemental Security Income (SSI)

Monthly Federal Payment Standard (dollars)
Individual ... 750
Couple ... 1,125

Cost-of-Living Adjustment (percent) ... 2.0

Resource Limits (dollars)
Individual ... 2,000
Couple ... 3,000

Monthly Income Exclusions (dollars)
Earned Income [a] ... 65
Unearned Income ... 20

Substantial Gainful Activity (SGA) Level for the Nonblind Disabled (dollars) ... 1,180

a. The earned income exclusion consists of the first $65 of monthly earnings, plus one-half of remaining earnings.

Office of Retirement and Disability Policy
www.socialsecurity.gov/policy

Produced and published at U.S. taxpayer expense

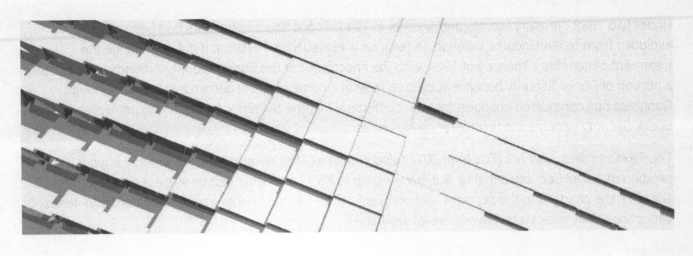

Chapter 6

Taxation of Social Security Benefits

Learning objectives

- Identify the threshold amounts of provisional income and determine what percentage, if any, of Social Security benefits are included in gross income for federal income tax purposes.

- Recognize that otherwise tax-exempt municipal bond interest is part of provisional income.

- Determine how Social Security Benefits of joint filers are taxed.

- Recognize sources of income that are generally not subject to federal income tax but are included in provisional income for purposes of determining the taxability of Social Security benefits.

- Recall the base amounts of provisional income used to determine the percentage of taxable Social Security benefits.

Overview

All types of benefits provided by Social Security, including disability benefits, may be subject to income tax. This is more likely to occur if the taxpayer receives these benefits in addition to other income, such as retirement plan distributions, wages, self-employment earnings, interest, dividends, or other taxable income. Although the types of income cited previously are generally reported on the recipient's Form 1040, tax-exempt income from municipal securities is also factored into calculating Social Security benefits taxation.

Under two 1938 Treasury Rulings and another in 1941, Social Security benefits had been specifically excluded from federal income taxation. (A revision was issued in 1970, but it did not change the treatment of benefits.) Then, as of 1984, with the enactment of the Social Security Amendments of 1983, a portion of Social Security became subject to federal income taxes, in certain instances. Although Congress has considered changes, for now, for federal income tax purposes, differing percentages of Social Security benefits are taxable, at various rates.

The Tax Cuts and Jobs Act (TCJA) of 2017 (also known as "Tax Reform") did not directly impact the taxation of Social Security benefits. But, because up to 85% of benefits can be subject to tax, as we will see later, the changes to the tax rates and brackets, as well as the changes to the standard and itemized deductions, may affect a taxpayer's overall tax liability.

How benefits are reported

Each January, those receiving Social Security benefits receive a *Social Security Benefit Statement* (Form SSA-1099) showing the amount of benefits paid in the previous year. This benefit statement is necessary for determining whether the benefits are subject to federal income tax.

Estimates or withholding

If a taxpayer owes taxes on Social Security benefits, he or she can make quarterly estimated tax payments to the IRS or elect to have federal taxes withheld from benefits.

Those receiving benefits are not required to have federal taxes withheld from their Social Security payments. However, they may find withholding more convenient than paying quarterly estimated tax payments. To have federal taxes withheld, or to change a withholding request, the recipient should

- complete IRS Form W-4V (*Voluntary Withholding Request*),
- select the percentage (7%, 10%, 12%, or 22%) of the monthly benefit amount to be withheld, and
- sign and return the form to a local Social Security office by mail or in person.

State and local taxes

The Social Security Administration (SSA) has no authority to withhold state or local taxes from benefit payments. Many states and local authorities do not tax Social Security benefits.

Provisional income

The amount of a Social Security benefit recipient's provisional income determines what percentage, if any, of benefits received are required to be included in that recipient's gross income for federal income tax purposes. Provisional income for purposes of Social Security taxation includes all items that are normally part of adjusted gross income (as previously mentioned), plus tax-exempt interest income, plus 50% of Social Security benefits. The 50% reflects that half of Social Security contributions were generally made by the taxpayer's employer(s), therefore not taxed.

Provisional income is sometimes called modified adjusted gross income.

Under current law (and lawmakers are seriously considering new rules), taxpayers are not subject to federal income tax on more than 85% of their Social Security benefits.

Base amounts

The following base amounts are used in figuring taxable Social Security:

Filing status	Base	Additional
Single	$25,000	$34,000
Head of household	$25,000	$34,000
Married filing jointly	$32,000	$44,000
Married filing separately	$0	
Qualifying widow(er)	$25,000	$34,000

If a taxpayer's provisional income is less than the base amounts for a particular filing status, then any Social Security benefits received are nontaxable entirely.

Example 6-1

Grandma Emma's only income is $1,500 per month in Social Security benefits; therefore, none of her benefits would be included in her gross income.

Example 6-2

Grandma's brother, Uncle Albert, has been a widower for the past 20 years. During his working years, he was a painter and provided art lessons in his studio. His income in retirement comes from only two sources. He receives $1,800 in monthly Social Security retirement benefits, and he is taking a required minimum distribution (RMD) of $500 per month from his individual retirement account. Uncle Albert's provisional income is calculated as follows:

IRA distribution	$6,000
½ Social Security	$10,800
Total provisional income	$16,800

Because Uncle Albert's provisional income is clearly lower than the $25,000 base that applies to single taxpayers, none of his Social Security retirement benefit is required to be included in his gross income for federal income tax purposes.

Example 6-3

Claude and Maude Iverson, a married couple, file their taxes jointly. Both Claude and Maude are receiving Social Security retirement benefits. Claude is receiving $1,000 per month, and Maude is receiving $300 per month. Additionally, Claude is receiving $1,000 per month from his former employer's money purchase plan and Maude is taking a required minimum distribution from her small IRA account of $4,800 for the year 2018. We can see that their provisional income is calculated as follows:

Claude's pension	$12,000
Maude's RMD	$4,800
½ of Claude's benefits	$6,000
½ of Maude's benefits	$1,800
Total	$24,600

Given that the Iverson's provisional income is less than the base of $32,000 that applies for married taxpayers filing jointly, none of their Social Security benefits are required to be included in their gross income.

The amount of taxable Social Security depends on a formula. If provisional income is more than the first base amount, up to 50% of Social Security is taxable. However, the taxable amount could be less. The same is true if provisional income exceeds the second base amount. Up to 85% of the Social Security is taxable, but the actual percentage could actually be less based on the formula. See the "Social Security Benefits Worksheet" of the Form 1040 instructions.

Therefore, an individual taxpayer having provisional income between $25,000 and $34,000 is required to include up to 50% of his or her benefits in gross income for federal income tax purposes. An individual taxpayer having provisional income more than $34,000 is required to report up to 85% of his or her benefits in gross income for federal income tax purposes. Married couples filing a joint return and having a combined provisional income that falls between $32,000 and $44,000, are required to report up to 50% of their combined benefits in gross income for federal income tax purposes. Married couples filing a joint return and having a combined provisional income of more than $44,000, are required to include up to 85% of their combined Social Security benefits in gross income for federal income tax purposes.

Example 6-4

Bob and Michelle Lofton, a retired married couple, are collecting Social Security retirement benefits. Michelle is receiving $2,000 per month in benefits and Bob is receiving $1,000 in benefits. Michelle is also receiving a monthly pension benefit from her former employer's pension amounting to $1,600 per month while Bob is taking RMDs from his IRA amounting to $600 per month. Additionally, the Loftons' received $30,000 in income from tax-exempt public-purpose municipal bonds in the 2018 tax year. Their year 2018 provisional income is as follows:

Michelle's pension	$19,200
Bob's IRA	$7,200
Municipal bond income	$30,000
½ Michelle's Social Security	$12,000
½ Bob's Social Security	$6,000
Total provisional income	$74,400

Clearly, the Loftons' provisional income is substantially higher than the $44,000 top threshold, which makes 85% of their Social Security retirement benefits includible in their gross income.

Married couples filing separately

Married couples who file separate tax returns have two different methods for computing the taxable portion of their Social Security benefits. For married couples who lived in the same household at any time during the year, their base amount is zero. Up to 85% of their benefits will be subject to tax. Married couples who lived apart for the entire year may use the base amount of $25,000 and the additional income amount of $34,000 for computing the taxable portion of their benefits.

Base amounts are not indexed

The thresholds for determining provisional income are not indexed for inflation since the law was instituted in 1983. Given that up to one-half of Social Security benefits are added to other income, it is likely that more and more middle-income clients and certainly higher-income clients will be including up to 85% of their Social Security benefits in gross income in the years to come if no changes are made to the tax law regarding Social Security benefits.

Retroactive benefits

A number of months can pass between the time a worker applies for Social Security disability benefits and when the worker can receive the first benefit payment. The first check will include any benefits due from the day when the worker applied for disability income benefits until the time when the disabled applicant was approved to receive benefits. This retroactive payment may be substantial. Further, the benefits might be subject to income tax for the year in which the payment was received. If an applicant paid an attorney to help in obtaining benefits, that cost is deductible.

Knowledge check

1. Regarding the taxation of Social Security benefits, which statement is correct?

    a. If the Social Security benefits will be taxable, the SSA is responsible to withhold and collect estimated tax on the payments.
    b. The taxpayer may elect to have federal income tax withholding on his or her Social Security benefits.
    c. The SSA generally will not withhold federal taxes from benefit payments because it is presumed that the taxpayer will make estimated quarterly payments.
    d. The SSA generally will not withhold federal taxes from benefit payments because the administrative burden is too great.

The lump-sum election

When a disabled individual receives his or her retroactive Social Security disability income (SSDI) payment, a portion of it may be attributable to prior tax years. Although the recipient is required to include the entire amount in gross income on the current year's tax return, there is an election that the taxpayer can make to recalculate prior years' taxes as if the payment had actually been received in those years.

If the as-if inclusion in prior years would reduce the taxable amount of the payment that the taxpayer received in the current year, it should be carefully considered.

Under the lump-sum election, determining taxes entails recalculating the disability income benefit recipient's tax returns from previous years. The taxpayer's Form 1099 from the SSA will include a breakdown of how much Social Security income is attributable to each year.

The process is to calculate the amount of tax that would have been paid each year as if the beneficiary had received the benefit amount indicated on his or her Form 1099, and then subtract the tax actually paid in those years. Next, add or subtract this result to the current year's tax return to determine tax liability.

In most cases, making the lump-sum election will be productive because it enables the taxpayer to offset the lump sum with a multiple of base amounts.

Amount of retroactive benefit

SSDI benefits may be paid retroactively to 12 months before the date of the application as long as the applicant's disability began on that date or earlier.

> ### Example 6-5
>
> Chuck became disabled on January 1, 2017, and filed his application on January 1, 2018. The benefits will be retroactive back to January 1, 2017. The actual amount that Chuck will receive is based on how much he paid in FICA tax while he was working.

Mini case

Joyce Foster is still adjusting both emotionally and financially to the death of her husband, Jim, in 2017. His life insurance policy named Joyce as sole beneficiary and provided a death benefit of $300,000. The Fosters have twin boys Rod and Todd, now age seven. Joyce is receiving a spouse's benefit of $1,500 per month as well as a children's benefit of $600, per child, per month.

Joyce invested the insurance proceeds in the Gibraltar Mutual Fund, which holds mainly common stocks. She has begun a systematic withdrawal program from the Gibraltar Fund account for $1,800 per month. The Gibraltar Fund provided Joyce with a Form 1099 reporting $15,000 in distributions for the year (part of the distribution was return of basis.) Although both Joyce's parents and Jim's parents are very generous to Joyce and the boys, Joyce has no other actual income. Let us have a close look at Joyce's provisional income for determining what percentage, if any, of her Social Security benefits would be included in her gross income for federal tax purposes.

Mutual fund income	$15,000
Half Joyce's Social Security	$9,000
Total provisional income	$24,000

Keep in mind that Joyce is now regarded as a single taxpayer with regard to applying the threshold amounts. Because her income does not exceed the $25,000 base for single Social Security benefit recipients, none of her Social Security benefits are taxable.

Joyce would not include the Social Security benefits attributable to her children Rod and Todd in her own provisional income although the benefit checks for the children are received by and made payable to her. If the twins had other income, one-half of their benefits would be combined with such income to determine whether provisional income was sufficient to trigger taxability of the children's benefits.

Knowledge check

2. Herman's claim for Social Security disability benefits was initially denied and later approved. He received retroactive benefits, some of which were attributable to the previous tax year and some of which are attributable to the current tax year. Regarding this lump-sum payment of retroactive benefits, what should Herman do?

    a. He must recognize the entire lump sum in the current tax year.
    b. He may elect to prorate the retroactive benefits between the current tax year and the prior tax year.
    c. He must prorate the retroactive benefits between the current tax year and the prior tax year.
    d. He may elect two-year income averaging for the retroactive Social Security lump-sum benefits.

Summary

The provisional income of the recipient of Social Security benefits determines what percent, if any, of those benefits are to be included in gross income for federal income tax purposes. Provisional income includes all income, including tax-exempt interest from municipal securities and, in many circumstances, workers' compensation benefits. The thresholds that determine the taxable percentage of Social Security benefits are not indexed for inflation. It is not unusual to see the maximum of 85% of Social Security benefits becoming subject to tax, due to the threshold amounts that subject them to taxation.

Retroactive disability benefits are generally taxed in the year in which they are received. However, an election is available that may generate a beneficial income tax outcome by attributing the tax to a prior year.

A surviving parent may receive benefit checks on behalf of his or her children (from the deceased parent's FICA contributions). That income is included in the provisional income of the child, rather than that of the surviving parent.

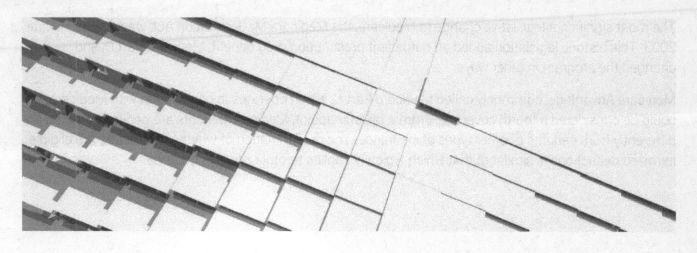

Chapter 7

Medicare

Learning objectives

- Recognize when a spell of illness begins, according to Medicare.

- Select the type of patient who is most likely to use up lifetime reserve days.

- Recall the percentage of a physicians' fees that Medicare Part B will cover. Identify what types of plans Medicare Part C plans most resemble.

- Recognize the type of benefits most likely to be excluded from a Medicare Supplemental (Medigap) insurance policy.

Overview

In addition to Social Security retirement and disability programs and Supplemental Security Income (SSI), the Social Security Administration (SSA) has operated the Medicare program since it became law in 1965. Medicare coverage is, with a few exceptions, available to older Americans beginning at age 65. It generally provides three distinct coverages.

Medicare Part A covers inpatient hospital services and certain out-of-hospital therapies. It also covers hospice care. Part B is more focused on doctors' fees and outpatient procedures.

The most significant legislative change to Medicare, the Medicare Modernization Act, was enacted in late 2003. This historic legislation added an outpatient prescription drug benefit, Medicare Part D, and changed the program in other ways.

Medicare Advantage, commonly called Medicare Part C, which operates in conjunction with Medicare, could be considered a fourth coverage. From a tax standpoint, Medicare benefits are generally treated no differently from benefits of other types of insurance. The determination of whether premiums are eligible itemized deductions is similar to that which typically applies to other health insurance.

Original Medicare

Medicare Parts A and B are sometimes called "Original Medicare." Original Medicare operates differently from private insurance plans like health maintenance organizations (HMOs). HMOs generally provide coverage (other than emergency care) only for services provided by doctors or hospitals in their network. Medicare generally allows the patient to visit any doctor or be treated in any hospital that accepts Medicare. Original Medicare operates under a "fee-for-service" arrangement, meaning that the doctor or hospital is paid for the services they actually provide.

Enrolling

Generally, an individual is automatically enrolled in Medicare Part A when that person attains age 65 and is receiving Social Security retirement benefits. Typically, the SSA mails one's Medicare card three months before the retirement benefit recipient's 65th birthday.

If an individual has employer-provided or other health insurance (or believes that he or she cannot afford the Medicare Part B premium) and wishes to elect out of Part B coverage, instructions included with the Medicare mailing will tell the recipient how to opt out.

Most people older than 65 don't pay a Part A premium because they paid Medicare taxes while working. However, for an individual not covered, or if the individual or spouse worked and paid Medicare taxes for less than 10 years total, a monthly Part A premium of $437 would apply in 2019. If an individual has 30 quarters of coverage but less than 40 quarters of coverage, a reduced premium of $240 is charged for coverage under Part A.

Medicare Part A hospital insurance

Medicare Part A (hospital insurance) covers hospital services, including semiprivate rooms (private rooms may be covered when such accommodation is medically necessitated), meals, general nursing care, prescription and other drugs administered in conjunction with inpatient treatment, and other hospital services and supplies. This includes care provided in acute care hospitals, critical access hospitals, inpatient rehabilitation facilities, long-term care hospitals, inpatient care as part of a qualifying clinical research study, and mental healthcare.

Requirements for coverage

Under Part A of Medicare, inpatient hospital care is covered if all the following conditions are satisfied:

- The patient's doctor orders inpatient hospital care to treat the patient's illness or injury.
- The patient requires the care that can be provided only in a hospital setting.
- The hospital accepts Medicare payments.
- The Utilization Review Committee of the hospital approves the patient's stay while that patient is hospitalized.

Inpatient costs associated with traditional Part A coverage

Although Medicare Part A covers a significant portion of inpatient hospital costs, the patient still retains exposure to costs. The benefit from Medicare Part A depends on how many days the patient stays in the hospital. The good news is that most studies report the average Medicare-covered inpatient hospital stay is eight days. That said, certain patients would be in the hospital considerably longer than average.

In 2019, for the first 60 days, the patient generally pays a deductible of $1,364 and Medicare pays the rest. After that, the longer the patient stays, the greater his or her exposure. Rather than the flat-dollar deductible that satisfies the patient's exposure during the first 60 inpatient days, the patient is then responsible for a daily copayment (copay). The patient pays $341 per day for days 61 through 90.

After inpatient day 90 and through day 150, a patient can tap into his or her store of nonrenewable lifetime reserve days. The patient must pay a copay of $682 per day until the 60 days of lifetime benefits have been used. After day 150, the patient is exposed to all the costs of inpatient care.

Example 7-1

Clara Goodwin, age 70, is covered under Medicare Part A. (Most likely, she is also covered under Medicare Part B, but that is mainly focused on her doctor bills. More on that later.) In June 2019, she suffers a serious bout with colitis, which results in severe bleeding and dehydration. She is hospitalized at Mercy General Hospital for four days. Presuming that Mercy General accepts Medicare payments, Clara's out-of-pocket exposure should not exceed $1,364.

Example 7-2

Hugh Stewart, age 88, underwent a quadruple cardiac bypass procedure. The procedure went poorly, and, in fact, it was difficult for the surgical team to get Hugh off the heart-lung machine. Hugh had to be intubated (on a ventilator or respirator) for 66 days after his surgery, during which time he remained in the intensive care unit of University Teaching Hospital. Given that Hugh is covered under Medicare Part A, his financial exposure for inpatient hospital care would be factored as follows:

Days 1 through 60	$1,364
Days 61 through 66 = $341 × 5	$1,705
Total	$3,069

Now, consider the less frequent situation in which a Medicare Part A insured patient dips into lifetime reserve days.

Example 7-3

Lillian Kozak, an 86-year-old widow, spent 130 days as an inpatient at Washington Hospital, much of which entailed intensive care. She died on the 130th day. The cost exposure that her estate would face is shown as follows:

Days 1 through 60	$1,364
Days 61 through 90 = $341 × 29	$9,889
Days 91 through 130 = $682 × 39	$26,598
Total	$37,851

Keep in mind that had Lillian still been hospitalized on day 151, her Medicare Part A benefit for inpatient care would have been exhausted.

Remember that the previously mentioned costs only reflect hospital care. The patient also has doctor bills to pay. Those are covered under Part B of Medicare.

Spell of illness

A *spell of illness* or benefit period is specifically defined. The patient is required to pay the inpatient deductible for every benefit period. A Medicare insured patient's first benefit period or *spell of illness* begins with the first night of a qualifying stay in a hospital.

Example 7-4

Duncan Miles, who is covered under Medicare Part A, suffers a fall at home on a Monday evening, fracturing his hip. His son calls 911 and Duncan is transported to the nearest emergency room at 10 p.m. At 3 a.m., the hospital decided to admit Duncan, so he can have the proper treatment to heal his fracture. Although Duncan entered the hospital on Monday night, his stay in the emergency room does not count toward his qualifying stay.

The spell of illness ends when the patient has not received any inpatient care (in the hospital or skilled nursing facility [SNF]) for 60 days in a row. There is no limit on the number of spells of illness that would be Medicare eligible. However, studies show that the average length of a hospital stay covered by Medicare is eight days.

Keep in mind that the Medicare-insured person does not have to use the entire 60 lifetime reserve days in one spell of illness; they can be allocated among several benefit periods. Nevertheless, the individual has a total of only 60 reserve days in his or her lifetime. Once the lifetime reserve days have been used, the beneficiary will receive coverage for only 90 days when the next spell of illness occurs.

Part A inpatient cost exposure summary

- Days 1–60: $1,364 deductible for each benefit period in 2019
- Days 61–90: $341 coinsurance per day of each benefit period in 2019
- Days 91 and beyond: $682 coinsurance per each lifetime reserve day after day 90 for each benefit period (up to 60 days throughout the patient's lifetime) in 2019
- Beyond lifetime reserve days, all costs

Blood transfusions

After the patient pays for the first three pints of blood donated by third parties, Medicare Part A pays 80% of any additional blood that is supplied to a hospital inpatient. In certain situations, the hospital obtains blood from a blood bank at no charge, and then, the patient is not obligated to pay for it or replace it. If the hospital must buy blood for an inpatient, that patient is required to either pay the hospital costs for the first three units of blood supplied within a calendar year or arrange for blood to be donated.

Psychiatric care under Medicare

Medicare Part A also pays for stays in psychiatric hospitals, but the benefit is limited to 190 days of inpatient care during a beneficiary's lifetime. Services may be provided either in a general hospital or a psychiatric hospital that only cares for patients suffering from mental health conditions.

In 2019, mental health inpatient stay benefits are covered as follows:

- $1,364 deductible for each benefit period
- Days 1–60: $0 coinsurance per day of each benefit period
- Days 61–90: $341 coinsurance per day of each benefit period
- Days 91 and beyond: $682 coinsurance per each "lifetime reserve day" after day 90 for each benefit period (up to 60 days over the patient's lifetime)
- Beyond lifetime reserve days: all costs
- 20% of the Medicare-approved amount for mental health services from doctors and other providers while a hospital inpatient

There is no limit to the number of benefit periods for mental healthcare that is provided in a general hospital. Multiple benefit periods have recently become available for mental healthcare in a psychiatric hospital. However, the lifetime limit of 190 days still applies.

Medicare premiums and coinsurance rates
Medicare Part A

Medicare Part A helps a covered individual pay the bills for several types of medical care, such as the following:

- Inpatient hospital care for up to 90 days each benefit period, plus 60 lifetime reserve days in a general hospital. It also covers up to 190 lifetime days in a Medicare-certified specialty psychiatric hospital.
- SNF care for up to 100 days in each benefit period. To qualify, the beneficiary must have been in the hospital for at least three consecutive days in the 30 days before admission and need skilled nursing services seven days a week, or physical, occupational, or speech therapy services five days a week.
- Home healthcare for up to 100 visits. To qualify, the beneficiary must have been in the hospital for at least three days in the 14-day period before receiving care and be homebound.
  - Under certain circumstances, coverage for home healthcare through Medicare Part B is available without a hospital stay.
- Hospice care. To qualify, a doctor must certify that the patient is terminally ill and has a life expectancy of less than 180 days.

What Medicare does not cover

Although Medicare provides a wide range of services, it generally would provide no benefit for the following:

- Acupuncture
- Cosmetic surgery
- Custodial (nonskilled) care in a nursing facility
- Most chiropractic care
- Non-emergency care outside the United States (Puerto Rico, the U.S. Virgin Islands, Guam, American Samoa, and the Northern Mariana Islands are considered part of the United States.)
  - Emergency room visits in foreign hospitals are typically covered when a foreign hospital is closer or easier to get to than the nearest United States hospital that can treat a covered individual's emergency.
- Dental care (Even dental care necessitated by an accident or medical procedure is not covered.)
- Experimental procedures. Medicare will not pick up the cost of any care deemed to be experimental.
- Eye exams and eyeglasses
- Hearing aids
- Hospital telephones or televisions
- Private nursing care

Parts A and B generally provide no benefit for outpatient prescription drugs. An exception may be available for certain outpatient chemotherapies.

State resources

If an older individual has limited income and resources, his or her state of residence may help pay for Part A and or Part B as well as for Medicare prescription drug coverage.

Current Medicare premiums and deductibles

Different Medicare premiums, deductibles, and coinsurance apply to specific parts of Medicare coverage.

Part A: (Hospital insurance) premium

If someone is not automatically covered for Medicare Part A, a premium of up to $437 each month applies in 2019. Most people have premium-free Part A coverage. Individuals entitled to such coverage starting at age 65 typically include those who

- already get retirement benefits from Social Security or the Railroad Retirement Board;
- are eligible to get Social Security or railroad benefits but have not applied for them yet; and
- had Medicare-covered government employment (or the spouse had).

Someone younger than age 65 may receive premium-free Part A coverage if he or she

- received Social Security or Railroad Retirement Board disability benefits for 24 months; or
- suffers from end-stage renal disease (generally meaning a dialysis patient) and meets certain requirements.

In most cases, an individual who chooses to buy Part A, is also required to carry Medicare Part B (medical insurance) and pay monthly premiums for both.

Part B: (Medical insurance) premium

Someone beginning Medicare coverage in 2019 or turning age 65 in 2019 will have a monthly premium of $135.50. However, if the insured individual's modified adjusted gross income (AGI) two years ago is more than a certain threshold, the premium is generally higher. The SSA will contact those required to pay more based on higher incomes. The amount of premium can change each year depending on the insured's AGI. Please refer to the following chart.

If yearly income in 2017 was			
File individual tax return	File joint tax return	File married and separate tax return	Insured pays (in 2019)
$85,000 or less	$170,000 or less	$85,000 or less	$135.50
more than $85,000 up to $107,000	more than $170,000 up to $214,000	not applicable	$189.60
more than $107,000 up to $133,500	more than $214,000 up to $267,000	not applicable	$270.90
more than $133,500 up to $160,000	more than $267,000 up to $320,000	not applicable	$352.20
more than $160,000 and less than $500,000	more than $320,000 and less than $750,000	above $85,000 and less than $415,000	$433.40
$500,000 and above	$750,000 and above	$415,000 and above	$460.50
Source: SSA			

Disagreeing with the charge

If one receives a notice to pay a higher amount for the Part B premium and he or she disagrees, one can apply for a review by submitting the *Income-Related Monthly Adjustment Amount—Life-Changing Event* form. However, it is clear from the preceding table that individuals and couples with AGIs that exceed certain inflation-indexed thresholds will pay more (sometimes substantially more). The amount of modified AGI for this purpose is that reported on the taxpayer's Form 1040 two years ago.

Late enrollment penalties

If an individual does not sign up for Part B when first eligible, a late enrollment penalty may apply. For each 12-month period during which an eligible individual delays enrollment in Medicare Part B, 10% Part B premium penalty applies, unless the applicant had insurance from his or her or the spouse's current job. Although an enrollee's Part B premium amount is based on income, the penalty is calculated based on the standard Part B premium. The penalty is then added to the beneficiary's actual premium amount for the rest of their lives.

Example 7-5

Anthony Howe turned 65 in 2013 and delayed signing up for Part B until 2019. His 2017 AGI was $95,000. (Assume that he did not have the employer insurance that enables delayed enrollment.) His monthly premium would be subject to a penalty, representing 60% (6 years × 10%) of the 2019 base amount for as long as he has Medicare. That penalty is added to the premium he is charged based on his 2017 income. Because Anthony's Medicare Part B premium is $189.60, his monthly premium with the penalty factored in would be $270.90 ($135.50 × 0.6 = $81.30 + $189.60).

Knowledge check

1. Due to a lifetime of savings, inheritances, and smart investing, Herbert, who is now a 78-year-old widower, has an annual AGI of $300,000. In 2019, what amount will he pay for his Medicare Part B premium?

    a. $135.50 per month.
    b. $270.90 per year.
    c. $433.40 per year.
    d. $433.40 per month.

Part B deductible

For most Americans, the 2019 Part B deductible is $185 for the year. These amounts have been inflation-indexed for some time. This means that once a Medicare beneficiary has paid $185 for medical care covered by Medicare Part B, Medicare will begin to pay for services at 80% of their approved amount. Certain services are paid at 100% by Medicare and not subject to the Part B deductible.

Therapy caps

In 2019, Medicare removed the caps that used to apply to physical, occupational, or speech/language therapy. Going forward, there are no caps on these therapies under current law.

Part D: Costs for Medicare drug coverage

Generally, people with Part D insurance pay premiums throughout the year into a Medicare drug plan. The monthly premiums operate in addition to the Part B premium.

Part D monthly premiums

The following chart shows 2019 estimated prescription drug plan monthly premiums based on AGI. If the insured's AGI is more than a certain threshold, an income-related monthly adjustment amount applies in addition to the Part D insurance premium.

The Part D monthly premium varies by plan (higher income consumers may pay more).

The following chart shows the estimated prescription drug plan monthly premium based on AGI as reported on the taxpayer's Form 1040 from two years ago. If such income is more than a certain limit, the Part D enrollee faces an income-related monthly adjustment amount in addition to the plan premium.

Filing status and yearly income in 2017 was			
File individual tax return	File joint tax return	File married and separate tax return	Filer pays (in 2019)
$85,000 or less	$170,000 or less	$85,000 or less	plan premium
more than $85,000 up to $107,000	more than $170,000 up to $214,000	not applicable	$12.40 + plan premium
more than $107,000 up to $133,500	more than $214,000 up to $267,000	not applicable	$31.90 + plan premium
more than $133,500 up to $160,000	more than $267,000 up to $320,000	not applicable	$51.40 + plan premium
more than $160,000 and less than $500,000	more than $320,000 and less than $750,000	more than $85,000 and less than $415,000	$71.90 + plan premium
$500,000 and above	$750,000 and above	$415,000 and above	$77.40 + plan premium

Source: SSA

Late enrollment penalty: A person who doesn't sign up for Part D when first eligible or someone who drops Part D and then gets it later may have to pay a late enrollment penalty for as long as he or she has Part D. The cost of the late enrollment penalty depends on how long the person went without creditable prescription drug coverage.

Deductibles

Deductibles vary substantially between Medicare drug plans. In 2019, no Medicare drug plan may have a deductible more than $415. Some Medicare drug plans do not impose a deductible.

- Initial deductible: Will be increased by $10 to $415 in 2019
- Initial coverage limit: Will increase from $3,750 in 2018 to $3,820 in 2019
- Out-of-pocket threshold: Will increase from $5,000 in 2018 to $5,100 in 2019
- Coverage gap (donut hole): Begins once the person reaches his or her Medicare Part D plan's initial coverage limit ($3,820 in 2019) and ends when he or she spends a total of $5,100 in 2019. In 2019, Part D enrollees will receive a 75% discount on the total cost of their brand-name drugs while in the donut hole. The 70% discount paid by the brand-name drug manufacturer will still apply to getting out of the "donut hole;" however, the additional 5% paid by the Medicare Part D plan will not count toward the out-of-pocket spending. Enrollees will pay a maximum of 37% co-pay on generic drugs while in the coverage gap.

Enrollees pay 5% of drug costs once in catastrophic coverage.   However, the insured retains some financial exposure due to

- copayments or coinsurance,
- costs in the coverage gap, and
- late enrollment penalty (if applicable).

Part D plan costs will vary depending on

- the drugs the patient uses,
- the plan selected,
- whether the drugs are dispensed by a pharmacy in the plan's network,
- whether the drugs the patient takes are on the plan's formulary, and
- whether the patient receives government subsidies for Medicare Part D costs.

Medicare Part D standard benefit model plan parameters

There are independent studies available that compare the standard benefit model plan parameters as released by the Centers for Medicare and Medicaid Services.[1]

The following table is a comparison of the standard benefit model plan parameters for plan years 2020 back through 2007.

---

[1] Source:

2020-2006 Medicare Part D Standard Benefit Model Plan Parameters table (https://q1medicare.com/PartD-The-MedicarePartDOutlookAllYears.php). Reprinted with permission.

Note: The 2020 defined standard Medicare Part D plan parameters shown online are only "proposed" at this time and have not been finalized by CMS. See the following article that summarizes the proposed changes to 2020 Medicare Part D plans: https://Q1News.com/742.html

Additional information is available from www.medicare.gov and CMS.gov.

Part D Standard Benefit Design Parameters:	2020	2019	2018	2017	2016	2015	2014	2013	2012	2011	2010	2009	2008	2007	2006
Deductible– After the Deductible is met, Beneficiary pays 25% of covered costs up to total prescription costs meeting the Initial Coverage Limit.	$435	$415	$405	$400	$360	$320	$310	$325	$320	$310	$310	$295	$275	$265	$250
Initial Coverage Limit– Coverage Gap (Donut Hole) begins at this point. (The Beneficiary pays 100% of their prescription costs up to the Out-of-Pocket Threshold)	$4,020	$3,820	$3,750	$3,700	$3,310	$2,960	$2,850	$2,970	$2,930	$2,840	$2,830	$2,700	$2,510	$2,400	$2,250
Out-of-Pocket Threshold– This is the Total Out-of-Pocket Costs including the Donut Hole.	$6,350	$5,100	$5,000	$4,950	$4,850	$4,700	$4,550	$4,750	$4,700	$4,550	$4,550	$4,350	$4,050	$3,850	$3,600

Part D Standard Benefit Design Parameters:	2020	2019	2018	2017	2016	2015	2014	2013	2012	2011	2010	2009	2008	2007	2006
Total Covered Part D Drug Out-of-Pocket Spending including the Coverage Gap — Catastrophic Coverage starts after this point. See note (1) below.	$9,038.75 (1)	$7,653.75 (1)	$7,508.75 (1)	$7,425.00 (1)	$7,062.50 (1)	$6,680.00 (1)	$6,455.00 (1)	$6,733.75 (1)	$6,657.50 (1)	$6,447.50 (1)	$6,440.00 plus a $250 rebate	$6,153.75	$5,726.25	$5,451.25	$5,100.00
Total Estimated Covered Part D Drug Out-of-Pocket Spending **including the Coverage Gap Discount (NON-LIS)** See note (2).	$9,719.38 plus a 75% brand discount	$8,139.54 plus a 75% brand discount	$8,417.60 plus a 65% brand discount	$8,071.16 plus a 60% brand discount	$7,515.22 plus a 55% brand discount	$7,061.76 plus a 55% brand discount	$6,690.77 plus a 52.50% brand discount	$6,954.52 plus a 52.50% brand discount	$6,730.39 plus a 50% brand discount	$6,483.72 plus a 50% brand discount					
Catastrophic Coverage Benefit:															
Generic/Preferred Multi-Source Drug (3)	$3.60 (3)	$3.40 (3)	$3.35 (3)	$3.30 (3)	$2.95 (3)	$2.65 (3)	$2.55 (3)	$2.65 (3)	$2.60 (3)	$2.50 (3)	$2.50 (3)	$2.40 (3)	$2.25 (3)	$2.15 (3)	$2.00 (3)
Other Drugs (3)	$8.95 (3)	$8.50 (3)	$8.35 (3)	$8.25 (3)	$7.40 (3)	$6.60 (3)	$6.35 (3)	$6.60 (3)	$6.50 (3)	$6.30 (3)	$6.30 (3)	$6.00 (3)	$5.60 (3)	$5.35 (3)	$5.00 (3)

Medicare Part D Benefit Parameters for Defined Standard Benefit
2006 through 2020 Comparison (continued)

Part D Full Benefit Dual Eligible (FBDE) Parameters:	2020	2019	2018	2017	2016	2015	2014	2013	2012	2011	2010	2009	2008	2007	2006
▪ Deductible	$0.00	$0.00	$0.00	$0.00	$0.00	$0.00	$0.00	$0.00	$0.00	$0.00	$0.00	$0.00	$0.00	$0.00	$0.00
▪ Copayments for Institutionalized Beneficiaries	$0.00	$0.00	$0.00	$0.00	$0.00	$0.00	$0.00	$0.00	$0.00	$0.00	$0.00	$0.00	$0.00	$0.00	$0.00

Maximum Copayments for Non-Institutionalized Beneficiaries

Up to or at 100% FPL:

▪ Up to Out-of-Pocket Threshold

	2020	2019	2018	2017	2016	2015	2014	2013	2012	2011	2010	2009	2008	2007	2006
- Generic / Preferred Multi-Source Drug	$1.30	$1.25	$1.25	$1.20	$1.20	$1.20	$1.20	$1.15	$1.10	$1.10	$1.10	$1.10	$1.10	$1.05	$1.00	$1.00
- Other Drugs	$3.90	$3.80	$3.70	$3.70	$3.60	$3.60	$3.60	$3.50	$3.30	$3.30	$3.30	$3.20	$3.10	$3.10	$3.00
▪ Above Out-of-Pocket Threshold	$0.00	$0.00	$0.00	$0.00	$0.00	$0.00	$0.00	$0.00	$0.00	$0.00	$0.00	$0.00	$0.00	$0.00	

Over 100% FPL:

▪ Up to Out-of-Pocket Threshold

	2020	2019	2018	2017	2016	2015	2014	2013	2012	2011	2010	2009	2008	2007	2006
- Generic / Preferred Multi-Source Drug	$3.60	$3.40	$3.35	$3.30	$2.95	$2.65	$2.55	$2.65	$2.60	$2.50	$2.50	$2.40	$2.25	$2.15	$2.00
- Other Drugs	$8.95	$8.50	$8.35	$8.25	$7.40	$6.60	$6.35	$6.60	$6.50	$6.30	$6.30	$6.00	$5.60	$5.35	$5.00
▪ Above Out-of-Pocket Threshold	$0.00	$0.00	$0.00	$0.00	$0.00	$0.00	$0.00	$0.00	$0.00	$0.00	$0.00	$0.00	$0.00	$0.00	$0.00

Medicare Part D Benefit Parameters for Defined Standard Benefit
2006 through 2020 Comparison (continued)

Part D Full Subsidy - Non Full Benefit Dual Eligible Full Subsidy Parameters:	2020	2019	2018	2017	2016	2015	2014	2013	2012	2011	2010	2009	2008	2007	2006
Eligible for QMB/SLMB/QI, SSI or applied and income at or below 135% FPL and **resources ≤ $9,230 (individuals in 2019) or ≤ $14,600 (couples, 2019) (4)**															
• Deductible	$0.00	$0.00	$0.00	$0.00	$0.00	$0.00	$0.00	$0.00	$0.00	$0.00	$0.00	$0.00	$0.00	$0.00	$0.00
• Maximum Copayments up to Out-of-Pocket Threshold															
- Generic / Preferred Multi-Source Drug	$3.60	$3.40	$3.35	$3.30	$2.95	$2.65	$2.55	$2.65	$2.60	$2.50	$2.50	$2.40	$2.25	$2.15	$2.00
- Other Drugs	$8.95	$8.50	$8.35	$8.25	$7.40	$6.60	$6.35	$6.60	$6.50	$6.30	$6.30	$6.00	$5.60	$5.35	$5.00
• Maximum Copay above Out-of-Pocket Threshold	$0.00	$0.00	$0.00	$0.00	$0.00	$0.00	$0.00	$0.00	$0.00	$0.00	$0.00	$0.00	$0.00	$0.00	$0.00

Partial Subsidy Parameters:	2020	2019	2018	2017	2016	2015	2014	2013	2012	2011	2010	2009	2008	2007	2006
Applied and income below 150% FPL and **resources between $14,390 (individual, 2019) or $28,720 (couples, 2019) (category code 4) (4)**															
• Deductible	$89.00	$85.00	$83.00	$82.00	$74.00	$66.00	$63.00	$66.00	$65.00	$63.00	$63.00	$60.00	$56.00	$53.00	$50.00
• Coinsurance up to Out-of-Pocket Threshold	15%	15%	15%	15%	15%	15%	15%	15%	15%	15%	15%	15%	15%	15%	15%

Partial Subsidy Parameters:	2020	2019	2018	2017	2016	2015	2014	2013	2012	2011	2010	2009	2008	2007	2006
▪ Maximum Copayments above Out-of-Pocket Threshold															
- Generic / Preferred Multi-Source Drug	$3.60	$3.40	$3.35	$3.30	$2.95	$2.65	$2.55	$2.65	$2.60	$2.50	$2.50	$2.40	$2.25	$2.15	$2.00
- Other Drugs	$8.95	$8.50	$8.35	$8.25	$7.40	$6.60	$6.35	$6.60	$6.50	$6.30	$6.30	$6.00	$5.60	$5.35	$5.00

(1) Total Covered Part D Spending at Out-of-Pocket Threshold for Non-Applicable Beneficiaries - Beneficiaries who ARE entitled to an income-related subsidy under section 1860D-14(a) (LIS)

(2) Total Covered Part D Spending at Out-of-Pocket Threshold for Applicable Beneficiaries - Beneficiaries who are NOT entitled to an income-related subsidy under section 1860D-14(a) (NON-LIS) and do receive the coverage gap discount. For 2020, the weighted gap coinsurance factor is 88.0579%. This is based on the 2018 PDEs (90.18% Brands & 9.82% Generics)

(3) The Catastrophic Coverage is the greater of 5% or the values shown in the chart above. In 2020, beneficiaries will be charged $3.60 for those generic or preferred multisource drugs with a retail price under $72 and 5% for those with a retail price greater than $72. For brand-name drugs, beneficiaries would pay $8.95 for those drugs with a retail price under $179 and 5% for those with a retail price over $179.

(4) This amount includes the $1,500 per person burial allowance. The resource limit may be updated during contract year 2019.

Are the premiums tax-deductible?

Subject to certain limitations, medical expenses have historically been deductible as an itemized deduction on the taxpayer's Schedule A. *Medical expenses* are generally described as any of the costs of diagnosis and treatment of an illness or injury, including medical supplies and equipment and preventive medical care. Allowable expenses also include some unexpected expenses such as the cost of transportation medical care (even if the taxpayer uses his or her own vehicle) and the cost of altering the taxpayer's home or installing special equipment for medical reasons.

A Medicare beneficiary can generally count the following as allowable medical expenses for purposes of claiming the Schedule A itemized deduction for medical expenses:

- Premiums for Part B, for Medicare private health plans and for Part D drug plans. If the taxpayer pays a premium for Part A, that is allowed as well.
- Premiums for Medigap supplemental insurance.
- Out-of-pocket costs for deductibles and copayments or coinsurance for Medicare Parts A, B, and D services.
- Out-of-pocket costs for prescription drugs in the Part D donut hole (coverage gap).
- Out-of-pocket costs for services Medicare does not generally cover, such as hearing aids, medically necessary eyeglasses and contact lenses, dental treatment, and nonmedical (custodial) nursing home care.
- Premiums for long-term care insurance (subject to certain limitations).

Costs that may not be deducted include the following:

- Premiums for group health insurance (such as employer-sponsored insurance) that are paid with pretax dollars
- Payments made for medical services that were paid by an insurer or any other source
- Late penalties added to Part B or Part D premiums
- Prescription drugs purchased from foreign sellers
- Nonprescription drugs, vitamins, and supplements—unless recommended by a physician to treat a specific medical condition

Of course, the typical taxpayer older than age 65 may deduct only those expenses exceeding the AGI threshold. Under the Tax Cuts and Jobs Act of 2017, total medical expenses must now exceed 7.5% of AGI to be deductible for tax year 2018. For future years after 2018, medical expenses must exceed 10% of AGI to be deductible.

Example 7-6

David Spear's income in the current year consists of Social Security retirement benefits, a small pension distribution, and some minimal bank interest. He is 67 years old. David's AGI is $30,000. Of that, 7.5% is $2,250. However, David's total allowable medical expenses for the year are $4,000. He would be able to deduct $1,750 ($4,000 minus $2,250). If, in this example, his medical expenses were less than $2,250, he could not claim any as a deduction.

Recall though, that younger individuals may receive Medicare benefits if they have been receiving Social Security disability income benefits for at least 24 months, or if they suffer from end-stage renal disease (dialysis patients). In that situation, and starting in tax year 2013, a 10% floor applies through the end of 2017 and again starting in 2019 and beyond.

Continuing with our example, had David, in the preceding situation, been 44 rather than 67 and the year was 2017, he would be able to deduct only $1,000 in eligible unreimbursed medical expenses because the first $3,000 of such expenses would represent 10% of his AGI.

Premium deductibility for self-employed people with Medicare insurance

Of course, not every American who turns age 65 immediately stops working. Individuals who work for themselves (and others) may work much longer. Medicare recipients who have self-employment income may deduct the premiums they pay for Medicare coverage—the same as premiums for any other type of health insurance by the self-employed. All Medicare premiums (Parts A, B, C, and D) are treated as *insurance* constituting medical care and may be deducted. Sole proprietors must pay the Medicare premiums directly.

Self-employed individuals for the purposes the deduction for AGI include sole proprietors, partners, and more-than-2% shareholders of an S corporation. The deduction from gross income is available for medical insurance paid during the tax year for self-employed individuals, their spouses, and their dependents, including their children younger than age 27.

No health insurance deduction in a loss year

If a self-employed taxpayer reports a loss from self-employed activities, then that individual may not deduct otherwise eligible health insurance costs because this above-the line deduction is limited by that taxpayer's self-employment income. In other words, the medical expense deduction cannot produce a net operating loss for a self-employed person.

Knowledge check

2. Blake is 70 years old. Are his Medicare premiums deductible from income?

    a. Yes, premiums are always deductible.
    b. No, premiums are never deductible.
    c. Yes, to the extent they (combined with other out-of-pocket qualifying medical expenses) exceed 7½% of his AGI.
    d. Yes, but only up to an annual maximum of $2,010.

Mini case study

Cheryl Sanchez is a married taxpayer, age 67. Her husband, Sal, is age 68 and a lifelong smoker. Sal had a very good year financially due to writing a situation comedy pilot that was picked up by a major television network. Cheryl continues to own and operate her restaurant, Chez Nacho, an unincorporated business. Because of some unexpected kitchen repairs, in 2018, Cheryl reports profits from Chez Nacho of only $8,000. Premiums for Medicare for herself and her husband first reflect the Medicare Part B monthly premium, which—based on their income of $300,000—is $352.20 per person, per month. For the two spouses, that amounts to $8,453. Additionally, they are paying $325 per month ($3,900 annually) for a Medigap F policy for Cheryl and $550 per month ($6,600 annually) for Sal who is "rated" because he is a smoker.

Total insurance costs follow:

Medicare Part B (both)	$ 8,453
Medigap (both)	$10,500
Total	$18,953

However, because Cheryl's self-employment income is only $8,000, their self-employed health insurance deduction on Form 1040 is limited to that amount ($8,000). Due to the 10% floor (.1 × $300,000 = $30,000), the Sanchezes would not be able to deduct the remaining $10,953 ($18,953 − $8,000) as an itemized deduction on Schedule A.

Skilled nursing care under Medicare Part A

Medicare Part A provides benefits for up to 100 days of inpatient care provided in an SNF. This is not custodial-type nursing home care that occurs when an elderly person becomes unable to complete daily living activities such as walking or eating independently. Medicare will provide no benefit for nursing home care unless such care is medically necessitated, physician ordered, and likely to improve the patient's condition. Once progress ceases, the patient is then no longer eligible for skilled services and therefore no longer eligible for Medicare skilled nursing benefits.

If a patient has been admitted to an SNF and is receiving Medicare-covered skilled nursing care, that person's prescriptions generally will be covered under Medicare Part A.

Medicare provides benefits for skilled care in a facility if both of the following conditions are satisfied:

- The beneficiary was first hospitalized for at least three days.

  To satisfy this requirement, the patient must have been admitted to the hospital as an inpatient before entering a Medicare-approved facility. Patients who are merely being "kept for observation" do not satisfy the three-day hospitalization requirement. Rehabilitative care will be provided for the same condition for which the patient was hospitalized.

- Admission to the SNF occurs within 30 days of discharge from the hospital.

As a practical matter, there is seldom a meaningful gap between hospital discharge and SNF admission. Typically, seniors who need rehabilitative services and treatment go directly from hospital discharge to the SNF.

Mini case

Estelle Edwards, age 79, had been very active. She enjoys playing tennis and traveling. Estelle, who lives alone, was a patient at an SNF for 100 days to help her recover from knee replacement surgery. She was discharged from the SNF after 100 days because she had run out of days in her benefit period.

Her SNF per diem was $452. For the first 20 days, Medicare would pay the entire cost for a total of $9,040. For the subsequent 80 days, Estelle would have to pay a copay of $170.50 for a total of $13,640. However, Medicare would pick up the extra $281.50 per day from day 20 up to day 100 for a total of $22,520.

Six weeks later Estelle fell and broke her right hip and was again admitted to the hospital where she required emergency surgery and will need rehabilitation. It is unlikely that Medicare would cover the SNF care she would need after she was discharged from the second hospital stay.

As discussed, Medicare covers up to 100 days of care at an SNF during each benefit period (days 1–20 in a benefit period are covered in full by Medicare; days 21–100 are covered with $170.50 per day in 2019). Estelle's benefit period started the day she entered the hospital the first time—for the knee replacement— and ends when she has not received Medicare-covered inpatient care at a hospital or SNF for 60 consecutive days. Clearly, Estelle has not been out of a hospital or SNF for 60 days in between her injuries, and thus does not qualify for a new benefit period. Because she has already spent 100 days in an SNF during this (original) benefit period, Medicare will provide no coverage for additional days in an SNF.

Estelle must pay the full cost of any additional days that she spends in the SNF unless she has another form of insurance to help pay those costs. If she cannot afford to pay the costs, Estelle should consider contacting her state's Medicaid program and learn whether she qualifies for assistance.

Home healthcare coverage *Under Medicare Part A*

If a patient was an inpatient in a hospital for three days or had been admitted to an SNF after a hospital stay, Medicare Part A covers the beneficiary's first 100 days of home healthcare. Medicare Part B covers additional days.

Regardless of whether the care is covered under Medicare Part A or Part B, Medicare pays the full cost. In other words, no deductible or copayment applies for home healthcare visits.

What services are covered?

If a patient is eligible for the Part A home health benefit, Medicare covers the following types of care:

- Skilled nursing services and home health services provided up to seven days a week for no more than eight hours per day and 28 hours per week (Medicare may cover up to 35 hours in certain unusual situations.)
- Skilled nursing care, which includes services and care that can be performed safely and effectively only by a registered nurse (RN) or a licensed practical nurse. Examples of skilled nursing care activities that Medicare would typically cover include injections (and teaching patients to self-inject), tube feedings, catheter changes, observation and assessment of a patient's condition, management and evaluation of a patient's care plan, and wound care.
- Medicare pays in full for a home health aide if the patient requires skilled services. A home health aide provides personal care services including help with bathing, using the toilet, and dressing. However, if the beneficiary needs only personal care, that individual will not qualify for the Medicare home care benefit.
- Medicare home healthcare under Part A provides a benefit for physical, speech, and occupational therapy services that can only be performed safely by or under the supervision of a licensed therapist and that are necessary for treating the patient's illness injury. Unlike the situation with skilled nursing care in a facility, there is no requirement that home healthcare visits ultimately improve the patient's condition.
  - Physical therapy includes gait training and supervision of and training for exercises to regain movement and strength to a body area.
  - Speech-language pathology services include exercises to regain and strengthen speech and language skills. Occupational therapy helps the patient to regain the ability to do usual daily activities such as eating and putting on clothes independently.
- Medicare pays in full for physician-ordered social services ordered to assist the (typically elderly) patient with social and emotional concerns related to that patient's illness. This might include counseling or help with identifying and engaging community resources.
- Medical supplies. Medicare pays in full for certain medical supplies provided by the Medicare-certified home health agency, such as wound dressings and catheters needed for the patient's care.
- Durable medical equipment. Medicare pays 80% of its approved amount for certain pieces of medical equipment, such as a wheelchair or walker. The patient is required to pay 20% coinsurance (plus up to 15% more if the home health agency providing services does not accept *assignment*—accept the Medicare-approved amount as payment in full).

When a patient's other needs for Medicare home health end, he or she may still be able to obtain occupational therapy under the Medicare home health benefit.

Creating a plan of care

At the start of home healthcare and when the patient's condition changes, the agency providing the home healthcare must conduct an in-person assessment to determine which kinds of services the patient will require. The home health agency is then required to develop a plan of care that indicates the type and amount of services that the Medicare beneficiary will need. The patient's physician must sign the plan of care soon after it starts and recertify that plan at least every 60 days. The plan of care and certification operates for a 60-day window. If the patient still needs more care going forward, the plan of care and certification can be renewed for as many 60-day periods as needed as long as the patient's doctor signs them. A face-to-face meeting is not required for recertification.

Mini case

Unfortunately, after being discharged from the hospital, Ruth Weller, age 85, is housebound. Ruth had enjoyed a reasonably active life before her hospitalization and had been a volunteer reader at her local library. After pulmonary surgery, she developed adult-onset diabetes, which required blood testing and insulin injections throughout the day. Ruth needs help managing her medications, and it is hoped that occupational therapy will improve her ability to walk and move in general. Ruth and her (adult) children had several meetings with the hospital's social services staff before she was discharged, and a home healthcare agency, Healing Hands, Inc. was engaged.

Within a day or so of Ruth's discharge, Flo Nightingale, an RN, was dispatched by Healing Hands, Inc. and visited Ruth in her home. Flo took her vital signs and asked Ruth many questions. She tried to assist Ruth in walking for a few steps. Flo determined that although Ruth is able to eat independently, preparing meals will be difficult for her. Flo then developed a home care plan for Ruth. Services she recommended included occupational therapy (walking), skilled nursing care (medications—especially mastering the self-injections), and a walker to help Ruth become steadier as she moves about. Flo also recommends Ruth meet with a social worker to explore affordable ways to find assistance with meal preparations or deliveries. Ruth's doctor approves Flo's plan. No more than 60 days later, Ruth will be reassessed to determine whether the current plan of care should continue, be altered, or be discontinued.

It is important for the patient's doctor to agree with the plan of care and is satisfied that the plan contains all the care that is appropriate for the patient. The plan of care is often contained in the same form as the home health certification that the patient's doctor must sign to indicate the need for Medicare home care. As part of the Medicare certification for home healthcare, the doctor must confirm that the patient had a face-to-face meeting with him or her, or, more typically, with a representative of the home healthcare agency providing the services. Although it typically occurs sooner, the assessment meeting must occur within 90 days of starting to receive home healthcare (in certain circumstances within 30 days after actual administration of home healthcare). The physician must certify to Medicare that the face-to-face meeting confirmed the patient is homebound and qualifies for intermittent skilled care.

The face-to-face encounter can also be accomplished through telehealth. In certain areas, Medicare will accept telecommunications (such as video conferencing).

Hospice coverage *Under Medicare Part A*

Hospice care is for people with a terminal illness who are expected to live six months or less. Coverage includes medication for relief of pain, and control of other symptoms; medical, nursing, and social services; and grief counseling.

More than 5,000 hospices participate in the Medicare program in the United States. From the first program that opened in 1974, hospice programs continue to grow and are located in all 50 states. The services must be provided by a Medicare-approved hospice. Hospice care is palliative care. This care is administered to make the dying patient physically and emotionally comfortable by managing pain and other symptoms. It is not intended to be curative. Such hospice programs also provide grief counseling to the patient and to the family.

Most hospice care is provided in the terminally ill patient's home, but inpatient care in a hospice facility, hospital, and nursing facility care can also be covered. However, Medicare will not cover any benefit for room and board for a terminally ill patient living at home or in a long-term care facility. The amount and types of care offered depends on the patient's condition. Medicare also will cover inpatient respite care, which is care that enables a patient's usual caregiver (typically a family member) to rest. Although the standard hospice benefit period is six months, Medicare will continue to cover a patient's hospice care as long as the hospice physician or the medical director of the hospice facility recertifies the patient to be terminally ill.

Costs associated with hospice care

Although there is no user cost for hospice services, the patient must pay a copayment of $5 for each outpatient prescription as well as 5% of the Medicare-approved amount for inpatient respite care. (This is not a fixed dollar amount, but rather what Medicare considers "reasonable" for hospice care in the region.)

For example, if Medicare pays $400 per day for inpatient respite care, the patient will pay $20 per day. Each time that a patient receives respite care, Medicare covers up to five days. There is no limit to the number of times that a person can receive respite care. Total copays for respite care should be no more than the inpatient hospital deductible amount for the year in which hospice care is elected—$1,364 in 2019.

Hospice care benefits under Medicare

In conjunction with hospice care under Medicare Part A, the following benefits are generally covered:

- Nursing services. Medicare pays in full for skilled nursing care services when they are delivered by or under the supervision of a licensed nurse. Administration of medications, tube feedings, catheter changes, observation and assessment of a patient's condition, management and evaluation of a patient's care plan, and wound care are all skilled nursing activities.
- Skilled therapy services. Medicare pays in full for physical, speech, and occupational therapy to manage symptoms or to help the patient carry out activities of daily living (for example, eating, walking, dressing, toileting).

- Home health aide services. Medicare pays in full for a home health aide to provide personal care services including help bathing, using the toilet or dressing, and certain homemaker services.
- Durable medical equipment and medical supplies. Medicare pays in full for durable medical equipment and medical supplies needed to relieve pain or manage a medical condition.
- Respite care (caregiver relief)
- Short-term inpatient care to manage symptoms and control pain. Medicare will cover short-term in-patient care in a hospice, hospital, or nursing facility only if the patient's pain and other symptoms cannot be managed elsewhere. This can occur when the caregiver cannot or will not provide the care that a patient needs in a home setting.
- Medical social services. Medicare pays in full for services from a social worker (under the direction of a doctor) that address the social and emotional concerns of the patient and family members that relate to the patient's terminal condition. This might include counseling or help in finding community resources.
- Prescription drugs. The Medicare hospice benefit covers only prescription drugs related to pain relief and symptom control. Inpatient prescription drugs are covered in full. The patient's financial exposure can be no more than $5 for each outpatient prescription filled that is prescribed for pain relief and symptom control.

Ultimately, a Medicare-covered patient must decide as to whether to have his or her condition managed toward a possible cure in a hospital setting or to receive palliative care in a hospital setting; Medicare will cover either, but not both types of care simultaneously.

Knowledge check

3. Gary is a fighter. Although he was certified to have a life expectancy of fewer than six months, he is still alive, albeit weak, 200 days after his hospice admission. What will Medicare do?

    a. Stop paying for Gary's care.
    b. Automatically continue Gary's hospice care.
    c. Increase Gary's co-payment for hospice care.
    d. Recertify Gary's condition as terminal, then continue his hospice benefits.

Medicare Part B coverage

Medicare Part B insurance covers costs associated with medically necessary services such as doctors' visits, outpatient care, home health services, and more. Part B also provides benefits for certain preventive services. Most Americans participate in Medicare Part B insurance.

Additionally, Medicare Part B provides benefits for the following:

- Physicians' visits received as an inpatient at a hospital or at a doctor's office, or as an outpatient at a hospital or other healthcare facility
- Medically necessary services or supplies that are needed for the diagnosis or treatment of a medical condition and meet accepted standards of medical practice (for example, laboratory tests, x-rays, physical therapy or rehabilitation services, and more)
- Ambulance services
- Some home healthcare (not otherwise covered under Part A)
  - If the patient is homebound and requires skilled care, there is no prior hospital stay requirement for Medicare Part B coverage of home healthcare.
  - There is no deductible or coinsurance for Part B covered home healthcare.
- Preventive services to prevent illness or detect it at an early stage, when treatment is most likely to work best (for example, pap tests, an annual flu shot, and colorectal cancer screenings)

Medical checkups

Medicare Part B covers two types of physical exams: one when the beneficiary first enrolls in Medicare and one each year after that. The SSA labels these as the initial "Welcome to Medicare" physical exam and the yearly wellness exam.

The 2010 Affordable Care Act created the once-a-year wellness visit as a new benefit, paying doctors to perform it and making it free to patients. Within six months of first providing the benefit in 2011, Medicare had paid for nearly 1 million "Welcome to Medicare" exams.

The annual wellness visit (AWV) takes place with one's primary care provider, is covered once every 12 months after the first year of Medicare coverage, and has no deductibles, coinsurance, or copayments.

The AWV includes the provider taking the enrollee's medical history, completing a health risk assessment, evaluating the patient's physical condition, and screening for cognitive impairment, including depression. It also includes a personalized prevention plan in which the doctor develops a strategy, along with the patient, to manage that person's health, including planning for the preventive services and screenings that an older person is likely to require within the next 5–10 years. The plan helps the beneficiary take advantage of Medicare's preventive services, many with no cost-sharing.

Part B cost exposures

The Medicare Part B insured has significant cost exposure. First, the Part B deductible applies. Then the patient must share in costs exceeding that amount. The patient (unless eligible for a needs-based subsidy) must typically pay 20% of the Medicare-approved amount of the service. The 20% exposure for doctors' fees can add up significantly. An individual may save by using doctors or providers who accept a Medicare assignment.

Example 7-7

Grandpa Stanley underwent quadruple cardiac bypass surgery. The surgeon's fee was $18,185, and the anesthesiologist's fee was $4,000. In addition to the $185 Part B deductible, Grandpa Stanley has to pay 20% of the total bills from the two doctors, or $4,400. Unfortunately, complications arose within a few days following Grandpa Stanley's surgery and a repair procedure was necessary. Total bills for the follow-up surgical procedure were $12,000. Grandpa Stanley is now responsible for another $2,400. His financial exposure for the two procedures is $6,985. For most retirees, this is a substantial cost and an uncomfortable situation. However, if Grandpa Stanley had acquired Medigap insurance (discussed later in this chapter), that insurance would have paid his inpatient costs.

Knowledge check

4. Which of the following is **not** covered by Medicare Part A?

    a. Hospital insurance.
    b. Hospice care.
    c. Physician-ordered rehabilitative care.
    d. Custodial nursing home care.

Medicare Part C Advantage plans

Medicare Part C is commonly called Medicare Advantage. Medicare Advantage programs are private plans run through Medicare that, by law, must be at least "equivalent" to regular Part A and Part B coverage. These programs are private Medicare-approved health plans for those individuals eligible for Medicare. When an individual enrolls in a Medicare Advantage Plan, he or she is still in Medicare. There are many variations in coverages and costs among Part C plans. Any given one may cover less of one cost and more of another than Parts A and B benefits do. Factors that affect the monthly premium depend on the insured's state of residence and the private insurer selected, as well as whether the Medicare Advantage coverage is provided through an HMO or PPO. These plans may help lower the costs of receiving medical services or provide extra benefits for an additional monthly fee.

How do Medicare Part C plans operate?

Medicare Advantage plans typically operate through a network of clinics, doctors, and hospitals. As with HMOs and (in a sense) PPOs, the patient must seek treatment from providers within that network. Most plans include prescription medication coverage. However, if an enrollee already has prescription drug coverage, a Medicare Advantage plan that does not include prescription drug coverage would be a better choice.

Although most Medicare Advantage plans offer full coverage within the network, they also cover emergency treatment while out of town. There are several different options to choose from within the Medicare Advantage plan. These can include the HMO plan, PPO plan, private fee-for-service plan, as well as a special needs plan.

The special needs Medicare Advantage plan covers those with special health needs as well as specific chronic health-related issues. If an individual chooses the special needs plan, it must include Parts A, B, and D. When comparing Medicare Advantage plans, it is wise to consider deductible and drug copays as well as plan premiums.

Medicare Part C eligibility

One must have eligibility for both Parts A and B to enroll in a Medicare Advantage plan. An individual can generally join if he or she

- lives in the service area of the plan which is applied for;
- has Medicare Part A and Part B coverage; and
- does not suffer from end-stage renal disease (permanent kidney failure requiring dialysis or a kidney transplant).

Additionally, the individual must not have a Medigap insurance policy.

Changing plans

Generally, a Medicare Part C enrollee will be able to change plans only once a year during the *annual election period*. The annual election period, also called the *open enrollment period*, is October 15– December 7.

Knowledge check

5. Which statement is **not** correct regarding Medicare Part B?

    a. Medicare Part B covers outpatient or doctor visits.
    b. Medicare Part B does not cover home healthcare.
    c. Medicare Part B provides coverage for an annual wellness visit.
    d. Medicare Part B covers an annual flu shot.

Medicare Part D — Prescription drugs

Any individual who is covered by Medicare (under either Part A or Part B) is entitled to drug coverage (known as Part D) regardless of income. No physical exams are required. The applicant cannot be denied for health reasons or because that person already requires several prescriptions.

Obtaining Part D coverage

A Medicare-insured person must enroll in one of the private insurance plans that Medicare has approved to provide it. Coverage is available through

- a "stand-alone" prescription drug plan (PDP) that offers only drug coverage. This is the typical choice of those who receive their other health benefits through the original Medicare fee-for-service program; or
- a Medicare Advantage prescription drug plan (MA-PD) that covers both medical services and prescription drugs. This approach provides all healthcare services in one package.

Medicare Part D costs

Under the standard benefit (the minimum set by law), over the course of a calendar year, the Medicare Part D-insured individual will pay the following:

- A monthly premium (amount varies among plans).
- An annual deductible (no more than $415 in 2019) before benefits are actually triggered.
- A share of the cost of each prescription (either a flat co-pay or a percentage of the cost) during the initial coverage period. This continues until the insured's total drug costs (those paid by both the insured and the plan) reach $3,820 in 2019 starting from the beginning of the year.
- A percentage of costs in the coverage gap after the initial coverage limit is exceeded. In 2019, the insured must pay 25% of his or her plan's price for brand-name drugs and 37% for generic drugs in the gap. The donut hole phases out when costs exceed $5,100 in 2019.
- No more than 5% of drug costs once in the catastrophic period of coverage. This begins after costs exceed $5,100 in 2019 and continues until the end of the calendar year.

Items that count toward the coverage gap
- The yearly deductible, coinsurance, and copayments
- The discount on brand-name drugs in the coverage gap
- What the insured pays in the coverage gap

Items that don't count toward the coverage gap
- The drug plan premium
- Pharmacy dispensing fee
- What the insured pays for drugs that aren't covered

Medicare Part D mini case

Retired nurse Edith Eldredge has reached the donut hole, or coverage gap, in her Medicare Part D plan. At her neighborhood pharmacy, the cost to fill one name-brand prescription medicine is $60 per month, plus a $2 dispensing fee. Edith will pay 25% of the cost for the drug and the dispensing fee or $15.50 ($62 × 25 = $15.50).

Although Edith pays $15.50, she is actually credited for $60.50 toward filling her coverage gap because the amount of the discount (required under the 2010 Affordable Care Act) as well as what Edith actually pays out of pocket count toward the donut hole. The remaining $1.50, which represents 75% of the $2 dispensing fee, is not counted toward her coverage gap.

Edith also has a generic prescription (and is still in the coverage gap). The price of the generic drug per month is $20, plus the $2 dispensing fee. After the 63% coverage is applied to the $22, Edith will pay $8.14 out of pocket for the generic prescription. The $8.14 brings her closer by that amount to closing her coverage gap.

With her two prescriptions, Edith is closing her coverage gap by $68.64 per month, and if she takes many different medications (as many elderly Americans do), she may close the donut hole entirely.

Late enrollment penalty

It is beneficial to enroll in Medicare Part D as quickly as possible after enrolling in Parts A or B (generally both) because an applicant will be penalized with an extra 1% of the national average premium for each month of delay without creditable coverage. The penalty (and average premium) increases each year in which the Medicare enrollee has no Part D coverage.

> ### Example 7-8
>
> Grace Gardner delays Part D enrollment for 20 months. Her Part D premiums will always be at least % more than the amount she would have paid had she signed up when she first enrolled in Medicare for the remainder of her life.

Avoiding the late enrollment penalty

Several situations will help a Medicare Part D enrollee avoid the late penalty.

- When an individual turns age 65, that person should generally join a Part D drug plan during the seven-month initial enrollment period following initial eligibility for Medicare Part A and Part B. This period runs from three months before the month of an individual's 65th birthday to three months after it.
- To avoid the premium penalty, if an individual's 65th birthday is August 20, he or she should join a Part D drug plan before the end of October at the latest (with coverage starting in December).

- When an individual becomes eligible for Medicare through collecting Social Security disability income benefits, that benefit recipient also has a seven-month period to sign up for Medicare Part D as well as Parts A and B. This period runs from three months before the 25th month in which Social Security disability benefits were paid and ends three months after it.
- When the Medicare-insured person loses prescription coverage from a current or former employer or union, the individual would not be subject to the late premium penalty if he or she enrolls in Part D insurance when losing the original coverage. This presumes that the prior plan provided benefits at as high a level as a Medicare Part D plan.
- When an individual no longer has prescription drug coverage under the Consolidated Omnibus Budget Reconciliation Act (COBRA), that person would not be subject to the late premium penalty if he or she enrolls in a Medicare drug plan within 63 days of COBRA drug benefits ending. This presumes that the prior plan provided benefits as generous as typical Medicare Part D programs do.

Other circumstances include release from prison (63-day enrollment window) and return from living abroad (three-month enrollment window.)

Knowledge check

6. Which of the following statements is **not** correct regarding Medicare Part C?

   a. Medicare Part C or Medicare Advantage plans generally operate as PPOs and HMOs.
   b. Medicare Part C or Medicare Advantage plans generally provide their services through network doctors and hospitals.
   c. Many, but not all, Medicare Advantage plans provide prescription drug coverage.
   d. Medicare Part C is primarily a prescription drug program that covers all outpatient prescription drugs.

Medicare supplemental (Medigap) insurance

Medicare supplemental insurance (Medigap), sold by private companies, can help pay some of the healthcare costs that original Medicare does not cover, for example, copayments, coinsurance, and deductibles. As many of our prior examples have demonstrated, these gaps can present substantial exposure to a Medicare-insured individual (typically, a retiree).

Certain Medigap policies also offer coverage for services that original Medicare does not cover, for example, medical care when a Medicare beneficiary is traveling outside the United States. If an individual is enrolled under original Medicare and then acquires coverage under a Medigap policy, Medicare will pay its share of the Medicare-approved amount for covered healthcare costs. Then the Medigap policy pays what it covers over and above the Medicare benefits.

An individual must pay the private insurance company a monthly premium for Medigap policy in addition to the monthly Part B premium that goes to Medicare.

Medigap policies sold after January 1, 2006, may not include prescription drug coverage. Those seeking prescription drug coverage should enroll in Medicare Part D. (An exception applies for individuals still carrying an H, I, or J Medicare supplemental policy that dates from before 2006.) It is illegal for an insurance producer to sell a Medigap policy to anyone who currently maintains a Medicare Medical Savings Account Plan.

Types of Medigap plans

Insurance producers must sell older Americans a standard plan and only one policy. Currently, there are several standard Medigap policies from which to choose. Medigap A is the most basic core policy. As one moves higher in the alphabet, the plans add more coverage. For example, Medigap E will offer one or more benefits not included in Medigap D, but will lack a benefit provided in Medicare F, and so on.

Because of mandated standardization, there is little difference in plans offered among different insurers. However, residents of Massachusetts, Minnesota, or Wisconsin should check with their state insurance departments if considering an insurance company that issues policies in those states because Medigap policies in those states offer coverage different from the models followed by the 47 other states.

For residents of these three states, Medigap policies are standardized in a different way. These residents have guaranteed issue rights to buy a Medigap policy, but the policies are different.

- *Massachusetts*—See https://www.medicare.gov/supplement-other-insurance/compare-medigap/massachusetts/medigap-massachusetts.html.
- *Minnesota*—See https://www.medicare.gov/supplement-other-insurance/compare-medigap/minnesota/medigap-minnesota.html.
- *Wisconsin*—See https://www.medicare.gov/supplement-other-insurance/compare-medigap/wisconsin/medigap-wisconsin.html.

Medigap policy benefits

All Medigap policies are required to include coverage for certain core benefits, such as copays for Part B services and extended stays in the hospital.

Example 7-9

Medicare pays 80% of the surgeon's $3,000 bill for Lou's hernia surgery. Under Medicare Part B, Lou's share would be 20% of $3,000 or $600. Medigap pays Lou's copay entirely. He pays nothing.

Under rules that took effect in 2010, the following table illustrates how the different standard forms of Medigap policies offered coverage.

Comparing Medigap coverages

The chart that follows shows basic information about the different benefits Medigap policies cover.

Legend:
Yes = the plan covers 100% of this benefit
No = the policy doesn't cover that benefit
% = the plan covers that percentage of this benefit
N/A = not applicable

Medigap Benefits	Medigap Plans									
	A	B	C	D	F*	G	K	L	M	N
Part A coinsurance and hospital costs up to an additional 365 days after Medicare benefits are used up	Yes	Yes	Yes	Yes	Yes	Yes	Yes	Yes	Yes	Yes
Part B coinsurance or copayment	Yes	Yes	Yes	Yes	Yes	Yes	50%	75%	Yes	Yes***
Blood (first 3 pints)	Yes	Yes	Yes	Yes	Yes	Yes	50%	75%	Yes	Yes
Part A hospice care coinsurance or copayment	Yes	Yes	Yes	Yes	Yes	Yes	50%	75%	Yes	Yes
Skilled nursing facility care coinsurance	No	No	Yes	Yes	Yes	Yes	50%	75%	Yes	Yes
Part A deductible	No	Yes	Yes	Yes	Yes	Yes	50%	75%	50%	Yes
Part B deductible	No	No	Yes	No	Yes	No	No	No	No	No
Part B excess charge	No	No	No	No	Yes	Yes	No	No	No	No
Foreign travel exchange (up to plan limits)	No	No	80%	80%	80%	80%	No	No	80%	80%
Out-of-pocket limit**	N/A	N/A	N/A	N/A	N/A	N/A	$5,560	$$2,780	N/A	N/A

* Plan F also offers a high-deductible plan. If you choose this option, this means you must pay for Medicare-covered costs up to the deductible amount of $2,300 before your Medigap plan pays anything.

** After you meet your out-of-pocket yearly limit and your yearly Part B deductible, the Medigap plan pays 100% of covered services for the rest of the calendar year.

*** Plan N pays 100% of the Part B coinsurance, except for a copayment of up to $20 for some office visits and up to a $50 copayment for emergency room visits that don't result in inpatient admission.

Starting January 1, 2020, Medigap plans sold to new people with Medicare won't be allowed to cover the Part B deductible. Because of this, Plans C and F will no longer be available to people new to Medicare starting on January 1, 2020. If you already have either of these 2 plans (or the high deductible version of Plan F) or are covered by one of these plans before January 1, 2020, you'll be able to keep your plan. If you were eligible for Medicare before January 1, 2020, but not yet enrolled, you may be able to buy one of these plans.

Common exclusions

No insurance policy will cover everything that is not covered by Medicare. Medicare excludes certain types of medical expenses—so do many Medicare supplement, Medicare select, Medicare cost policies, and Medicare Advantage plans.

Services typically excluded under these policies include the following:

- Custodial care in nursing homes
- Private-duty nursing care
- Eyeglasses
- Hearing aids
- Dental care
- Cosmetic surgery
- Prescription drugs (policies issued after 2006)

Obtaining Medigap coverage

If a senior citizen age 65 or older purchases a Medigap policy within six months of enrolling in Part B, full federal guarantees and protections are provided. This means that a Medigap insurer cannot reject an applicant or charge a higher premium because of current or past health problems. Further, the policy must cover preexisting medical conditions.

However, in certain situations, an insurer may delay coverage of treatment for a preexisting condition for a period, typically six months, after purchase. Some state laws give additional consumer protections relative to preexisting conditions.

There are several other situations in which a Medigap insurance applicant is entitled to these protections—such as losing employer health coverage, COBRA, or retiree benefits that function as secondary coverage after Medicare. These protections also generally apply for individuals enrolled in a Medicare Advantage plan that closes down or if the Advantage plan insured out of its service area. In these circumstances, the period for buying a Medigap policy with full guarantees is about two months.

For persons younger than 65 who have Medicare entitlement due to disability, these federal guarantees do not apply, although many states mandate similar protections.

Free-look period

All states require a 30-day "free look" period. After someone buys Medicare supplemental insurance (Medigap), he or she has 30 days from the date when the policy is delivered to review it. If the buyer decides to decline the policy within this period, the company must refund all the premiums.

Continuing the coverage

The federal government mandates that standardized Medigap policies must be "guaranteed renewable" even if the insured's health worsens. Guaranteed renewable means that the insurance company may not cancel someone's Medigap coverage as long as he or she pays the premium in a timely manner. However, the insurance company generally retains the right (which it is likely to exercise) to raise premiums for its people with Medigap insurance.

Individual coverage

A Medigap policy covers only one person. Therefore, spouses must buy separate policies. However, premium discounts may be available if a couple buys two policies from the same insurance carrier. A Medigap policy differs from a Medicare Advantage Plan. Medigap policy essentially supplements one's original Medicare benefits. A person who obtains Medicare coverage through a Medicare Part C— Medicare Advantage plan cannot own a Medigap insurance policy.

Summary

This section provided a detailed explanation of the coverages and costs associated with Medicare insurance. Although Medicare Part A is hospital insurance, it also provides benefits for hospice care and physician-ordered rehabilitative care in an SNF. Part A also provides up to 100 home health visits with Part B covering any additional calls. The main emphasis on Part B coverage is physicians' fees and outpatient services. Medicare Part B also provides an annual wellness visit and certain types of preventive care such as screenings and an annual flu shot.

Medicare Part C describes Medicare Advantage plans, which generally operate as PPOs and HMOs generally providing their services through network doctors and hospitals. Many, but not all, Medicare Advantage plans provide prescription drug coverage. Medicare Part D is a prescription drug program that dovetails private insurance policies with Medicare coordination. Medicare Supplemental Insurance, commonly called Medigap insurance is commercially issued insurance that operates to pay patient costs for which Medicare does not pay benefits.

Benefits from health insurance programs are generally not taxable. Premiums for Medicare insurance and for Medigap insurance are deductible in the same manner that applies to other types of medical insurance premiums—as a Schedule A itemized deduction, subject to an AGI floor for most taxpayers, and as an above-the-line deduction for self-employed taxpayers, partners, and S corporation owners with greater than 2% equity.

Note, however, that the Tax Cuts and Jobs Act of 2017 repealed the overall limitation on itemized deductions through 2025.

Miscellaneous itemized deductions: All miscellaneous itemized deductions subject to the 2% floor under prior law are repealed through 2025 by the act.

Medical expenses: The act reduced the threshold for deduction of medical expenses to 7.5% of adjusted gross income for 2017 and 2018.

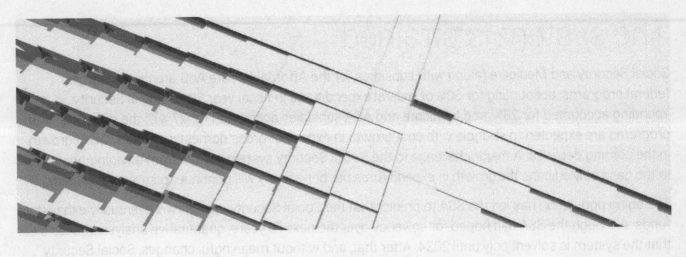

Chapter 8

The Future of Social Security and Medicare

Learning objectives

- Identify conventional wisdom on the future of Social Security and Medicare.

- Recognize official Social Security and Medicare concerns based on reports.

- Recall the effect of longer lifespans on the predicted shortfall in the Medicare system.

- Recognize the effect that the rules under the Patient Protection and Affordable Care Act (Affordable Care Act or ACA) have on Medicare costs.

Overview

When Social Security was established in 1935, a person who had attained age 65 had a 12-year life expectancy. Today, the average 65-year-old has a life expectancy of 20 years, according to the National Center for Health Statistics.

In 1950, 16.5 workers paid in retirement benefits for each retiree. According to reports from the Social Security Administration (SSA), in the year 2030, the ratio will be approaching only two workers paying in retirement benefits for each retiree. By then, the burden of taxes on each worker may well be unmanageable.

This section will examine what is occurring in both Social Security and Medicare trust funds and explore ways to address expected and worrisome shortfalls.

The system is strained

Social Security and Medicare (along with subsidies for the Affordable Care Act) are the two largest federal programs, accounting for 50% of federal expenditures in fiscal year 2017. Social Security spending accounted for 23%, and Medicare and ACA subsidies accounted for 27% of the spending. Both programs are expected to struggle with cost growth in excess of gross domestic product (GDP) growth in the coming decades. A major challenge to the Social Security system comes from an aging population. In the case of Medicare, the growth in expenditures per beneficiary will continue to strain the system.

The aging population has led the SSA to predict that the Social Security system will eventually exhaust its funds. Although the SSA had hoped for solvency over the next 75 years, quantitative analysis makes clear that the system is solvent only until 2034. After that, and without meaningful changes, Social Security would be funded to pay only about 78% of promised benefits.

Inadequate personal retirement savings

Amid this, Americans are woeful about retirement savings. Few workers save enough to make up for the loss of traditional guaranteed pensions that have frequently been replaced by less certain arrangements, such as 401(k) plans. According to a recent government accountability office (GAO) study, Americans ages 55–64 have retirement savings of $104,000.[1]

This will leave many retirees heavily reliant on Social Security, which currently pays a modest benefit; on average, $1,461 a month. Most retirees, with annual incomes up to $32,600, receive two-thirds to 100% of their postretirement income from Social Security.

Americans with incomes of up to $57,960 count Social Security as the largest component. Only the top fifth of seniors, with incomes of more than $57,960, do not rely on Social Security as their largest source of income. Even in this income group, Social Security represents about 20% of their annual income. Many in that classification are still working.

What Social Security has to say

The trustees of the Social Security and Medicare trust funds are required to report on the current and projected financial status of both programs on an annual basis (https://www.ssa.gov/OACT/TR/2018/index.html).

According to their report, the long-run actuarial deficits of the Social Security and Medicare programs decreased in 2017. The actuarial deficit in the Medicare hospital insurance program grew mainly because the trustees incorporated recommendations of the 2010–2011 Medicare Technical Panel to increase long-run health cost growth rate assumptions. Simultaneously, however, investment returns did not increase.

---

[1] See https://www.gao.gov/products/GAO-18-111SP.

The actuarial deficit in Social Security remained the same mainly because of the adjustment for updated economic data and assumptions.

Under current projections, the annual cost of Social Security benefits expressed as a share of workers' taxable earnings will grow from 13.81% in 2018 to roughly 17.0% in 2039 and will then increase slightly through 2092.

As expected, the trustees reported that neither Medicare nor Social Security will be able to sustain projected long-run program costs under current financing methods. Their findings propose that legislative modifications are necessary to avoid benefit shortfalls for beneficiaries.

Rapid change is necessary

The report indicates that if Congress acts sooner rather than later, more options and more time will be available to phase in changes, giving the public adequate time to prepare.

Concerns regarding Social Security

Both Social Security and Medicare will likely experience cost growth substantially in excess of GDP growth through the mid-2030s due to

- rapid population aging caused by the large baby-boom generation entering retirement and generations with lower birth rates entering employment, and
- growth in Medicare expenditures per beneficiary exceeding growth in per-capita GDP.

Social Security's total income is projected to exceed its total cost through 2021 as it has since 1982. The 2016 surplus of total income relative to cost was $35 billion. However, when interest income is excluded, Social Security's cost is projected to exceed its noninterest income throughout the projection period as it has since 2010. The trustees project that this annual noninterest deficit will average about $85 billion between 2018 and 2020. It will then rise steeply as income growth slows to its sustainable trend rate as the economic recovery is complete, while the number of beneficiaries continues to grow at a substantially faster rate than the number of covered workers.

After 2020, interest income and redemption of trust fund asset reserves from the General Fund of the Treasury will provide the resources needed to offset Social Security's annual deficits until 2034 when the reserves will be depleted. Thereafter, scheduled tax income is projected to be sufficient to pay about three-quarters of scheduled benefits through the end of the projection period in 2092. The ratio of reserves to one year's projected cost (the combined trust fund ratio) peaked in 2008, declined through 2016, and is expected to decline steadily until the trust funds are depleted in 2034.

The money source

Redemption of trust fund assets from the general fund of the Treasury will be necessary in order to provide the resources needed to offset Social Security's annual cash flow shortfalls. Because these redemptions will be lower than interest earnings through 2021, nominal trust fund balances will continue

---

to grow. A temporary reduction in the Social Security payroll tax rate reduced payroll tax revenues by $103 billion in 2011 and by $112 billion in 2012. The legislation establishing the payroll tax reduction also provided for transfers of revenues from the general fund to the trust funds in order to reasonably replicate payments that would have occurred if the payroll tax reduction had not been enacted. Those general fund reimbursements comprised about 15% of the program's noninterest income in 2011 and 2012.

Deficits are worrisome

Costs display a slightly different pattern when expressed as a share of GDP. Program costs equaled 4.9% of GDP in 2018, and the trustees project these costs will increase to 6.1% of GDP by 2038, decline to 5.9% of GDP by 2052, and thereafter rise slowly, reaching 6.1% by 2092.

The projected 75-year actuarial deficit for the combined old-age and survivors and disability insurance (OASDI) Trust Funds is 2.84% of taxable payroll, up from 2.83% projected in last year's report.

The Bipartisan Budget Act of 2015 was projected to postpone the depletion of Social Security Disability Insurance (SSDI) Trust Fund by six years, to 2022, largely by temporarily reallocating a portion of the payroll tax rate from the Old-Age and Survivors Insurance (OASI) Trust Fund to the SSDI Trust Fund. The effect of updated programmatic, demographic, and economic data extends the SSDI Trust Fund reserve depletion date by 10 years to 2032, in this year's report due to less filings for disability benefits since 2010. Although legislation is needed to address all Social Security's financial imbalances, the need remains most pressing with respect to the program's disability insurance component.

By law, the OASI and SSDI trust funds are separate entities. However, to summarize overall Social Security finances, the trustees have traditionally emphasized the financial status of the hypothetical combined trust funds for OASI and SSDI. The combined funds satisfy the trustees' test of short-range (10-year) close actuarial balance. The trustees project that the combined fund asset reserves at the beginning of each year will exceed that year's projected cost through 2022. However, the funds fail the test of long-range, close actuarial balance.

Knowledge check

1. By when does the SSA's analysis presume that the OASDI system will be inadequately funded?

    a. In 75 years.
    b. 2037–2050.
    c. 2034.
    d. 2027.

Medicare

The Medicare hospital insurance (HI) Trust Fund that supports Part A faces depletion earlier than the combined Social Security trust funds (although not as soon as the Disability Insurance Trust Fund when separately considered). Although the projected HI Trust Fund's long-term actuarial imbalance is smaller than that of the combined Social Security trust funds (under the assumptions employed in this report), funding concerns are significant.

The trustees project that total Medicare costs (including both HI and supplementary medical insurance or SMI expenditures) will grow from approximately 2.1% of GDP in 2016 to 3.4% of GDP by 2037 and will increase gradually thereafter to about 3.7% of GDP by 2091.

Deficit projections

The trustees project that the HI Trust Fund will be depleted in 2026, three years sooner than projected in last year's report. At that time, dedicated revenues will be sufficient to pay 91% of HI costs. The trustees project that the share of HI cost that can be financed with HI dedicated revenues will decline slowly to 78% in 2039 and will then rise gradually to 85% in 2092. HI expenditure is projected to exceed noninterest income throughout the projection period as it has in every year since 2008. The HI fund again fails the test of short-range financial adequacy because its trust fund ratio is already less than 100% of annual costs and is expected to decline in a continuous fashion until reserve depletion in 2026.

The HI Trust Fund's projected 75-year actuarial deficit is 0.82% of taxable payroll, which amounts to 0.4% of GDP through 2092, or 21% of noninterest income, or 17% of program cost. This estimate is up from 0.64% of taxable payroll projected in last year's report. This estimate reflects a 0.01 percentage point increase in the HI actuarial deficit that would have been expected if nothing had changed other than shifting the valuation period forward one year to 2017 through 2091, and a 0.17 percentage point decrease due to new data and changed assumptions.

To clarify, benefits are not simply distributed from a trust fund filled with income-producing assets. Unlike private sector pension funds, benefits are paid out of tax revenues. The trust funds essentially operate as accounting devices. As the trust funds draw down assets, general revenues (tax revenues in addition to the payroll taxes earmarked for these programs) transfer into the trust funds to redeem bonds that had previously been placed there during years when revenue from the payroll tax exceeded costs.

Challenges in a low return environment

The current Social Security trust fund contains only Treasury securities. Returns on Treasury securities have reached historic lows. The worsening of HI long-term finances is principally due to the adoption of short-range assumptions and long-range cost projection methods recommended by the 2010–2011 Medicare Technical Review Panel. Use of those methods increases the projected long-range annual growth rate for Medicare's costs by 0.3 percentage points. The new assumptions increased projected short-range costs, but those increases are offset, temporarily, by a roughly 2% reduction in 2013–2021 Medicare outlays required by the Budget Control Act of 2011.

Part B is more solid

For SMI, the trustees project that both Part B (which pays doctors' bills and other outpatient expenses) and Part D (which pays for prescription drug coverage) will remain adequately financed into the indefinite future because current law provides financing from general revenues and beneficiary premiums each year to meet the next year's expected costs. However, the aging population and rising healthcare costs cause SMI projected costs to grow steadily from 2.2% of GDP in 2017 to approximately 3.4% of GDP in 2039 and then more slowly to 3.7% of GDP by 2092. General revenues will finance roughly three-quarters of these costs and premiums paid by beneficiaries almost all the remaining quarter. SMI also receives a small amount of financing from special payments by states and from fees on manufacturers and importers of brand-name prescription drugs.

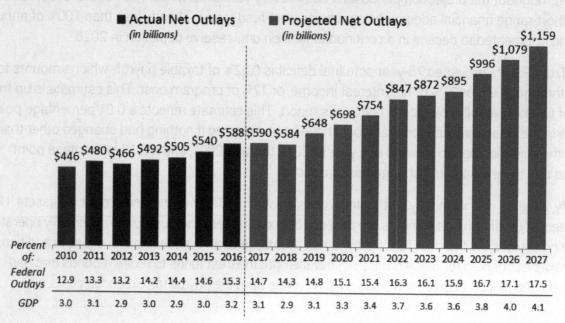

Actual and Projected Net Medicare Spending, 2010-2027

Percent of:	2010	2011	2012	2013	2014	2015	2016	2017	2018	2019	2020	2021	2022	2023	2024	2025	2026	2027
Federal Outlays	12.9	13.3	13.2	14.2	14.4	14.6	15.3	14.7	14.3	14.8	15.1	15.4	16.3	16.1	15.9	16.7	17.1	17.5
GDP	3.0	3.1	2.9	3.0	2.9	3.0	3.2	3.1	2.9	3.1	3.3	3.4	3.7	3.6	3.6	3.8	4.0	4.1

NOTE: All amounts are for federal fiscal years; amounts are in billions and consist of mandatory Medicare spending minus income from premiums and other offsetting receipts.
SOURCE: Congressional Budget Office, An Update to the Budget and Economic Outlook, 2017 to 2027 (June 2017).

Impact of the Affordable Care Act

Projected Medicare costs over 75 years are substantially lower than they otherwise would be because of provisions in the Patient Protection and Affordable Care Act, as amended by the Health Care and Education Reconciliation Act of 2010 (the Affordable Care Act or ACA). Most of the ACA-related cost saving is attributable to a reduction in the annual payment updates for most Medicare services (other than physicians' services and drugs) by total economy multifactor productivity growth, which the trustees project will average 1.1% per year.

In recent years, U.S. national health expenditure (NHE) growth has slowed considerably. There is uncertainty regarding the degree to which this slowdown reflects the impact of the recent economic conditions and other nonpersistent factors, as opposed to structural changes in the healthcare sector that may continue to produce cost savings in the years ahead. It is possible that U.S. healthcare practices are becoming more efficient as new payment models develop and providers anticipate less rapid growth of reimbursement rates in both the public and private sectors than has occurred during the past several decades.

The ACA's cost-reduction provisions were designed to create substantial savings. Notwithstanding the assumption of a substantial slowdown of per capita health expenditure growth, the projections indicate that Medicare still faces a substantial financial shortfall that will need to be addressed with further legislation. Such legislation should be enacted sooner rather than later to minimize the impact on beneficiaries, providers, and taxpayers.

It remains to be seen what additional action the current administration will take that might affect the ACA, Medicare, and other aspects of the healthcare industry.

Budgetary concerns

The drawdown of Social Security and HI Trust Fund reserves and the general revenue transfers into SMI will result in mounting pressure on the federal budget. In fact, pressure is already evident. The Medicare Modernization Act (2003) requires that the board of trustees determine each year whether the annual difference between program cost and dedicated revenues (the bottom four layers of exhibit 8-3) under current law exceeds 45% of total Medicare cost in any of the first seven fiscal years of the 75-year projection period. If so, the annual trustees report must include a determination of "excess general revenue Medicare funding." The trustees made that determination every year from 2006 through 2013, but because the difference between program cost and dedicated revenues is not expected to exceed the 45% threshold during fiscal years 2014–2020, there is no such determination in the current report.

Exhibit 8-3 Medicare cost and non-interest income by source as a percentage of GDP

Chart C—Medicare cost and non-interest income by source as a percentage of GDP

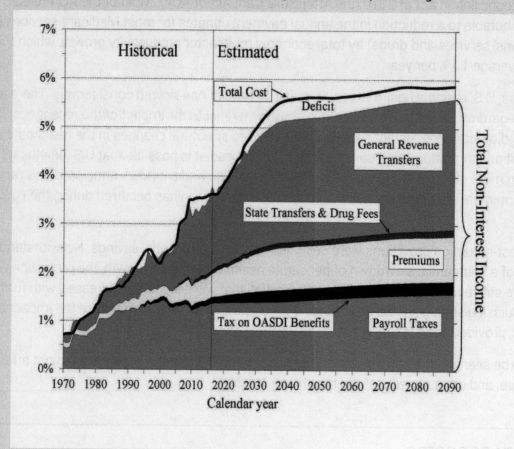

Fixing the problems

The politics

From its beginnings in 1935, politicians saw Social Security as a means to remove people from the workforce. It is noteworthy that Social Security was passed during the Great Depression when unemployment was high. The demand for jobs exceeded the supply.

Over time, Congress enacted rules to support this viewpoint. For example, workers had to retire to get all of their Social Security retirement benefits. If they continued to earn income, they would lose part of their payments.

In 1950, Congress exempted retirees age 75 and older from income limitation. That threshold was lowered to 72 in 1954 and 70 in 1983. The law that prevails now is the 2001 Freedom to Work Act, which ended the earnings limit for those at full retirement age (currently age 66) and older.

Current proposals

Legislation has been introduced in the Senate and House of Representatives, in each of the past few years. The legislation has not been voted on, but the following is a list of many ideas proposed to fix the problems:

- Increase the Social Security benefit computed by its existing formula by 1% per year until the increase gets to 15%. The idea here is to give all Social Security recipients a permanent increase in Social Security benefits above the cost of living adjustment (COLA).
- Use CPI-E, the consumer price index for elderly consumers rather than the current CPI. The CPI-E has greater weight given to housing and medical costs. On average over the past 30 years, the CPI-E has run about 0.3% higher than the CPI-W currently used.
- Give a minimum benefit to any worker who has worked for 10 years or more. The increased benefit would be 6.25% of the National Average Wage Index (NAWI) for someone with 11 years of employment and rising on a sliding scale to the maximum 125% of the NAWI for someone employed for 30 years or more.
- Raise or eliminate the ceiling of wages subject to Social Security withholding. The 2019 wage limit for Social Security withholding is $132,900. The proposal would tax wages for Social Security similar to taxation of wages for Medicare, which currently has no upper limit.
- Create another bend point in the PIA formula at 10%. A new 10% bend point would reduce the Social Security benefits calculated for high earners.
- Raise the retirement age for full retirement age (FRA) benefits to age 69 by 2030. The 1984 legislation raised the FRA to age 67 for those born in 1960 and later. People born in 1960 were 24 years old when they learned they would need to work longer for full Social Security benefits and gave them plenty of time to plan. The proposal to raise the FRA to 69 by 2030 would affect people who are currently 57 years old.
- Remove the earnings test for people between age 62 and FRA. Social Security benefits could begin at the reduced age 62 rate but a worker would not have to pay back benefits if they earned more than

the current limit of $17,040. A worker between age 62 and FRA pays back $1 of Social Security benefits for each $2 earned above the current limit of $17,640.

- Use chained CPI-W rather than CPI-W in computing annual COLA adjustments. Using chained CPI-W would reduce the annual increases in Social Security benefits each year.
- Stop children's Social Security benefits at age 15 rather than the current age 18. Lowering the age that children qualify for Social Security benefits would reduce the payments going out of the Social Security funds.
- Gradually increase the Social Security tax rate from its current 6.2% to 7.4% by the year 2042. An increase in the percentage of tax being withheld from workers' pay would increase the revenues being collected for Social Security.

How chained CPI works

The chained CPI assumes that people alter what they put in their shopping baskets due to price changes. For example, when beef becomes more expensive, Americans tend to eat less beef and buy more chicken, which is cheaper.

According to the U.S. Bureau of Labor Statistics, chained CPI is designed to be a closer approximation to a cost-of-living index than other CPI measures. The bureau is the agency that currently calculates and reports the CPI each month. It does not endorse one inflation measure over another.

Using chained CPI, Social Security's COLAs would reflect a lower inflation rate than the current CPI-W calculations.

Conclusion

With the availability of traditional pensions declining and the prospect of longer lifespans, uncertainty regarding Social Security benefits should be a motivating factor in encouraging Americans to begin and maintain a meaningful retirement plan; one that also includes adequate healthcare protection at all ages.

Knowledge check

2. Which would be most likely to decrease the shortfalls in the Social Security and Medicare systems?

   a. Eliminate the taxable wage base.
   b. Lower the taxable wage base.
   c. Repeal the Medicare tax on unearned income.
   d. Permit pharmaceutical companies to charge Medicare enrollees full retail price for prescription drugs.

Summary

The OASDI program—which for most Americans means Social Security—is the largest income-maintenance program in the United States. The long-term future of Medicare and Social Security is uncertain, triggering concerns for the many workers who are now paying into the system. Ideas being explored as potential fixes to the problems include raising or eliminating the taxable wage base, raising the full retirement age, means testing, and more. Making changes to Social Security and Medicare appears to always be on the table as part of deficit reduction strategy proposals.

No doubt, the future of Social Security will continue to be a major political and social issue for the foreseeable future.

Appendix A

FACT SHEET

Fact Sheet
SOCIAL SECURITY

2019 SOCIAL SECURITY CHANGES

Cost-of-Living Adjustment (COLA):

Based on the increase in the Consumer Price Index (CPI-W) from the third quarter of 2017 through the third quarter of 2018, Social Security and Supplemental Security Income (SSI) beneficiaries will receive a 2.8 percent COLA for 2019. Other important 2019 Social Security information is as follows:

Tax Rate	2018	2019
Employee	7.65%	7.65%
Self-Employed	15.30%	15.30%

NOTE: The 7.65% tax rate is the combined rate for Social Security and Medicare. The Social Security portion (OASDI) is 6.20% on earnings up to the applicable taxable maximum amount (see below). The Medicare portion (HI) is 1.45% on all earnings. Also, as of January 2013, individuals with earned income of more than $200,000 ($250,000 for married couples filing jointly) pay an additional 0.9 percent in Medicare taxes. The tax rates shown above do not include the 0.9 percent.

	2018	2019
Maximum Taxable Earnings		
Social Security (OASDI only)	$128,400	$132,900
Medicare (HI only)	No Limit	
Quarter of Coverage		
	$1,320	$1,360
Retirement Earnings Test Exempt Amounts		
Under full retirement age	$17,040/yr. ($1,420/mo.)	$17,640/yr. ($1,470/mo.)
NOTE: One dollar in benefits will be withheld for every $2 in earnings above the limit.		
The year an individual reaches full retirement age	$45,360/yr. ($3,780/mo.)	$46,920/yr. ($3,910/mo.)
NOTE: Applies only to earnings for months prior to attaining full retirement		

Social Security National Press Office   Baltimore, MD

age. One dollar in benefits will be withheld for every $3 in earnings above the limit.		
Beginning the month an individual attains full retirement age.	None	

	2018	2019
Social Security Disability Thresholds		
Substantial Gainful Activity (SGA)		
Non-Blind	$1,180/mo.	$1,220/mo.
Blind	$1,970/mo.	$2,040/mo.
Trial Work Period (TWP)	$ 850/mo.	$ 880/mo.
Maximum Social Security Benefit: Worker Retiring at Full Retirement Age		
	$2,788/mo.	$2,861/mo.
SSI Federal Payment Standard		
Individual	$ 750/mo.	$ 771/mo.
Couple	$1,125/mo.	$1,157/mo.
SSI Resource Limits		
Individual	$2,000	$2,000
Couple	$3,000	$3,000
SSI Student Exclusion		
Monthly limit	$1,820	$1,870
Annual limit	$7,350	$7,550
Estimated Average Monthly Social Security Benefits Payable in January 2019		
	Before 2.8% COLA	**After 2.8% COLA**
All Retired Workers	$1,422	$1,461
Aged Couple, Both Receiving Benefits	$2,381	$2,448
Widowed Mother and Two Children	$2,797	$2,876
Aged Widow(er) Alone	$1,348	$1,386
Disabled Worker, Spouse and One or More Children	$2,072	$2,130
All Disabled Workers	$1,200	$1,234

Index

SOCIAL SECURITY AND MEDICARE: MAXIMIZING RETIREMENT BENEFITS

BY THEODORE J. SARENSKI, CPA.PFS, CFP™

Solutions

The AICPA publishes *CPA Letter Daily*, a free e-newsletter published each weekday. The newsletter, which covers the 10-12 most important stories in business, finance, and accounting, as well as AICPA information, was created to deliver news to CPAs and others who work with the accounting profession. Besides summarizing media articles, commentaries, and research results, the e-newsletter links to television broadcasts and videos and features reader polls. *CPA Letter Daily*'s editors scan hundreds of publications and websites, selecting the most relevant and important news so you don't have to. The newsletter arrives in your inbox early in the morning. To sign up, visit smartbrief.com/CPA.

Do you need high-quality technical assistance? The AICPA Auditing and Accounting Technical Hotline provides non-authoritative guidance on accounting, auditing, attestation, and compilation and review standards. The hotline can be reached at 877.242.7212.

Solutions

Chapter 1

Knowledge check solutions

1.
   a. Correct. Social Security was enacted in 1935.
   b. Incorrect. Medicaid was created by the Social Security Act Amendments of 1965, which added Title XIX to the Social Security Act.
   c. Incorrect. SSI began in 1974.
   d. Incorrect. Medicare began in 1965.

2.
   a. Incorrect. The Medicare portion of FICA tax applies to unlimited amounts of wages.
   b. Correct. The taxable wage base operates to limit the OASDI portion of FICA tax.
   c. Incorrect. The Medicare portion of FICA tax applies to unlimited amounts of wages.
   d. Incorrect. The taxable wage base has nothing to do with discrimination in FICA taxation.

3.
   a. Incorrect. IRA distributions are not considered in determining the amount of unearned income to which the new 3.8% tax on unearned income applies.
   b. Incorrect. Form 1099 income is earned income. The 3.8% Medicare surtax applies to unearned income.
   c. Correct. Long-term capital gain is considered in determining the amount of unearned income to which the new 3.8% tax on unearned applies.
   d. Incorrect. IRC Section 121 applies to the exclusion of gains on homes sales not exceeding $250,000 or $500,000 (on a joint return).

Chapter 2

Knowledge check solutions

1.
   a. Incorrect. Six credits were the minimum amount to have fully insured status.

   b. Incorrect. Thirteen credits are not a minimum number of credits for any status of coverage.

   c. Correct. After 40 credits, the worker is permanently and fully insured and eligible for all (nondisability) benefits including retirement benefits.

   d. Incorrect. One hundred eighty credits are not a minimum number of credits for any status of coverage.

2.
   a. Incorrect. Form K-1 is used to report "pass-thru" income.

   b. Incorrect. Form 1099 SSC doesn't exist.

   c. Correct. Form W-2 is used to report an employee's Social Security earnings to the Social Security Administration.

   d. Incorrect. Form 1099-Misc is used to report various types of income to the IRS.

3.
   a. Incorrect. The credits must be earned in the period beginning with the quarter after the quarter he or she turned 21 and ending with the quarter he or she became disabled.

   b. Incorrect. Generally, a FICA-covered worker obtains disability-insured status if he or she earned at least 20 QCs during the last 10 years and has attained fully insured status. Exceptions apply for those under age 31 and in certain other cases.

   c. Correct. Workers who have not yet turned 31 will be fully insured if they have credits in at least one-half of the calendar quarters during the period beginning with the quarter after the quarter they turned 21 and ending with the quarter they became disabled.

   d. Incorrect. Generally, a FICA-covered worker obtains disability-insured status if he or she earned at least 20 QCs during the last 10 years and has attained fully insured status.

Chapter 3

1.
   a. Incorrect. Age 60 is the earliest age for widower benefits.
   b. Incorrect. Age 65 is the FRA/NRA for workers born in or before 1937.
   c. Incorrect. Age 66 is the FRA/NRA for workers born 1943–1954.
   d. Correct. The FRA/NRA for workers born in or after 1960 is age 67.

2.
   a. Incorrect. Clark's benefit will be reduced because he claims the benefit prior to his FRA/NRA.
   b. Correct. Clark's retirement benefit will be reduced by $5/9$ of 1% for each month of benefits paid before his FRA/NRA. His benefit will be reduced by 20%.
   c. Incorrect. The $5/12$ of 1% reduction for each month of benefits paid before his FRA/NRA only applies if Clark claims benefits more than 36 months prior to his FRA/NRA.
   d. Incorrect. Clark's retirement benefit will be reduced by $5/9$ of 1% for each month of benefits paid before his FRA/NRA. His benefit will be reduced by 20%.

3.
   a. Incorrect. Clara may not claim both benefits. Clara may claim 50% of Robert's PIA because it is higher than her own benefit.
   b. Incorrect. Clara may claim 50% of Robert's PIA because it is higher than her own benefit.
   c. Correct. Clara may claim 50% of Robert's PIA because it is higher than her own benefit.
   d. Incorrect. There is no reduction for early retirement because she waited until her FRA/NRA to claim benefits.

4.

   a. Correct. The statement is incorrect. Actuarially, the Social Security administration determined that the average person would ultimately receive the same amount of benefits from the time they start to their death under each of these scenarios. A person can receive a reduced Social Security benefit at age 62, a full benefit at age 66 (currently), or an enhanced benefit by waiting as long as to age 70.

   b. Incorrect. The statement is correct. Social Security benefits are increased by a certain percentage (depending on date of birth) if a fully insured worker delays retirement beyond full retirement age. The benefit increase no longer applies once the potential benefit recipient reaches age 70, even if the fully insured worker continues to delay taking benefits. When, from family history, a fully insured worker anticipates a long lifespan, delaying benefits, of course, would be more economically productive.

   c. Incorrect. The statement is correct. There are many reasons why the majority of older Americans choose to take Social Security retirement benefits prior to their normal retirement age. The early benefits carry present value, and the breakeven analysis often makes the argument unless the benefit recipient will lead a very long life.

   d. Incorrect. The statement is correct. The earliest age a fully covered worker can begin getting Social Security retirement benefits is 62. Many Americans are forced by necessity to take benefits as soon as they become eligible. Their benefits will be permanently lowered by this decision, but cash flow needs ultimately drive the decision to claim early benefits. According to the Social Security Administration, approximately 74% of retired workers claimed their benefits earlier than full retirement age.

Chapter 4

Knowledge check solutions

1.

   a. Incorrect. Kim is not eligible because she is in college.

   b. Incorrect. Tim is not eligible because he is married.

   c. Correct. To be eligible for survivor benefits as the child of a deceased worker, the child must be younger than 19, unmarried, and a high school student; or younger than 18 and no longer a student.

   d. Incorrect. Slim is not eligible because he is too old.

2.

a. Correct. Having a child in care is a basic requirement for some benefits, including spouse's benefits for a spouse younger than age 62 and for mother's and father's benefits. According to the Social Security Administration, "in care" means exercising parental control and responsibility for the welfare and care of a child younger than age 16 or a mentally disabled child aged 16 or older; or performing personal services for a physically disabled child aged 16 or older.

b. Incorrect. To be entitled to widow or widower's child in care benefits, constant supervision is not required.

c. Incorrect. To have a child in care means that the deceased worker's widow or widower is exercising parental control and responsibility for the welfare and care of the child, not supporting the educational needs of the deceased's child.

d. Incorrect. The deceased worker's widow or widower need not provide all physical care for the deceased's child. To have a child in care means that the deceased worker's widow or widower is exercising parental control and responsibility for the welfare and care of the child.

3.

a. Incorrect. The three-month period refers to another rule, where an exception is available if the deceased worker died within three months of an accident or died while on active duty in the armed services. There a survivor benefit may be available for a younger surviving spouse if that survivor is caring for a child aged 16 or younger.

b. Correct. An application for an ongoing monthly Social Security death benefit should be filed within six months of the worker's death. This is because no more than six months' worth of benefits will be paid retroactively.

c. Incorrect. The nine-month period refers to another rule. There is a survivor benefit potentially available for a younger surviving spouse if that survivor is caring for a child aged 16 or younger. The general rule is that to qualify for this benefit, the surviving spouse had to have been married to the deceased spouse for at least nine months.

d. Incorrect. Eighteen months' retroactive payments to survivors may go back only six months.

Chapter 5

Knowledge check solutions

1.

    a. Incorrect. Disability benefit payments start only after the applicant has been disabled for five months.

    b. Correct. Disability benefit payments start after the applicant has been disabled for five months, then continue until the benefit recipient's condition has improved to the level that he or she is able to return to work.

    c. Incorrect. This is the trial work period for persons who are working while collecting disability benefits.

    d. Incorrect. This period refers to one who has been collecting disability benefits for 24 months, after which time a beneficiary may become eligible for Medicare.

2.

    a. Correct. The number of Social Security credits or quarters that a disabled applicant needs to qualify for disability benefits depends on the age at which the applicant becomes disabled. Generally, an applicant needs 40 credits, 20 of which were earned in the last 10 years ending with the year in which the disability started.

    b. Incorrect. This is a reference to the rule for younger workers. For applicants before age 24, a disabled applicant may qualify having earned six credits in the three-year period ending when the disability begins.

    c. Incorrect. This rule refers to applicants who are age 24 to 31. A disabled applicant may qualify having credits attributable to working half the time between age 21 and when the disability commences.

    d. Incorrect. The general eligibility requirement for Social Security disability income benefits is 40 credits, 20 of which were earned in the last 10 years ending with the year in which the disability started. For applicants 31 or older, in general, the disabled applicant must have earned 20–40 work credits, depending on age. Unless the applicant is blind, he or she must have earned at least 20 of the credits in the 10 years immediately preceding the onset of disability.

3.

a. Correct. According to the Social Security Administration, an applicant must suffer from a medical condition that meets the Social Security Administration's definition of disability. SSDI benefits are eligible only to those with a severe, long-term, total disability. Total disability means the inability perform any substantial gainful activity for at least one year.

b. Incorrect. The inability of the insured to perform the tasks associated with the job at which he or she was employed when the disability began is one factor in considering disability. However, SSDI benefits are eligible only to those with a severe, long-term, total disability. The fact that the condition interferes with work-related tasks, refers to "severity" not to the issue of total disability. Total disability means the inability of the insured to perform any gainful employment; not just one's last means of employment.

c. Incorrect. This fact alone will not constitute total disability. The impairment or combination of impairments must be of such severity that the applicant is not only unable to do his or her previous work but cannot, considering his or her age, education, and work experience, engage in any other kind of substantial gainful work which exists in the national economy.

d. Incorrect. The fact that one's doctor may have advised someone not to work, or that he or she feels too ill to work, does not necessarily mean that the SSA will consider that individual to be disabled.

4.

a. Incorrect. The five-month period refers to the rule that disability benefit payments start after the applicant has been disabled for five months, then continue until the benefit recipient's condition has improved to the level that he or she is able to return to work.

b. Incorrect. When there is a real possibility that a claimant's condition may improve, in typical circumstances, Social Security reviews whether his or her disability benefits should continue every three years or fewer.

c. Correct. Most claims are set for review every three or seven years, depending on the likelihood that a benefit recipient's condition will improve. If a claimant has a condition that is expected to medically improve, a CDR may be conducted even sooner than three years.

d. Incorrect. This period refers to Social Security beneficiaries whose condition is not expected to improve or are disabled due to a permanent condition (such as a lost limb or impaired intellectual functioning). In those cases, claims may be reviewed even less than every seven years.

5.

a. Incorrect. Although it is true that disability benefits generally stop because of a person's medical improvement or work at the substantial gainful activity level, they will generally not stop immediately.

b. Incorrect. There is an additional grace period of two months—not one month—after the month of notice, in which the recipient will continue to get benefits.

c. Correct. Following a notification that a claimant is no longer eligible for Social Security disability income benefits, such benefits continue through a two-month grace period that follows the month of notice.

d. Incorrect. The general rule is that a claimant is no longer considered as disabled for purposes of receiving disability benefits in the month in which the cessation notice is mailed to the benefit recipient. Presuming that the recipient does not request a continuation of benefits, then his or her benefits will continue during the disability cessation month and the following two-month grace period.

Chapter 6

Knowledge check solutions

1.

a. Incorrect. In the absence of an election, the Social Security Administration is not responsible to withhold and collect estimated tax on the payments. A taxpayer may elect to have federal income tax withholding on his or her Social Security benefits.

b. Correct. The taxpayer may elect to have federal income tax withholding on his or her Social Security benefits.

c. Incorrect. There is no presumption that the taxpayer will make estimated quarterly payments. If the taxpayer elects to have federal income tax withholding on his or her Social Security benefits, the Social Security Administration will withhold federal income tax as requested.

d. Incorrect. If the taxpayer elects to have federal income tax withholding on his or her Social Security benefits, the Social Security Administration will withhold federal income tax as requested. The Social Security Administration is not absolved of its duty because the administrative burden is too great.

2.

    a. Incorrect. Herman is not required to recognize the lump-sum benefit in a single tax year because it is not attributable to a single tax year. Herman may elect to prorate the retroactive benefits between the current tax year and the prior tax year. He is not required to do so.

    b. Correct. Herman may elect to prorate the retroactive benefits between the current tax year and the prior tax year.

    c. Incorrect. There is no requirement to prorate the retroactive benefits between the current tax year and the prior tax year. He may, however, elect to do so.

    d. Incorrect. Two-year income averaging is not available in conjunction with retroactive Social Security disability income insurance payments. Herman may elect to prorate the retroactive benefits between the current tax year and the prior tax year. He is not required to do so.

Chapter 7

Knowledge check solutions

1.

    a. Incorrect. Taxpayers with much lower AGIs than Herbert would pay the minimum premium of $134 per month. Herbert's AGI is substantially more than the single taxpayer threshold that increases his Medicare Part B premium to $428.60 per month.

    b. Incorrect. The $268 figure represents the premium that would be paid by an individual with income of between $107,000 and $133,500 (for individuals) and between $214,000 and $267,000 for those filing a joint return.

    c. Incorrect. The $428.60 figure is correct, but Herbert's Medicare Part B premium is $428.60 per month, not year.

    d. Correct. Herbert's AGI is substantially more than the single taxpayer threshold that increases his Medicare Part B premium to $428.60 per month.

2.

    a. Incorrect. Medicare premiums may be deductible; but only if they reach certain thresholds.

    b. Incorrect. Subject to certain limitations, medical expenses are generally deductible as an itemized deduction on the taxpayer's Schedule A. A Medicare beneficiary can generally count premiums for Part A, Part B, Medicare private health plans, and Part D drug plans as allowable medical expenses for purposes of claiming the Schedule A itemized deduction for medical expenses.

    c. Correct. Medicare premiums are aggregated with other medical expense and long-term-care premiums as well as eligible unreimbursed medical expenses to the extent that they exceed 10% of the taxpayer's AGI (7½% for taxpayers age 65 and older through 2016 and again starting in 2018). Blake is age 70.

    d. Incorrect. The $2,010 cap refers to the annual per beneficiary therapy cap amount for physical therapy and speech language pathology services.

3.

    a. Incorrect. Although the maximum benefit period for hospice care is generally 180 days, if the patient is living but still certified as terminal, the hospice benefits will continue in normal amounts until the patient dies (or improves).

    b. Incorrect. Hospice care does not automatically continue unless a physician recertified a patient after six months.

    c. Incorrect. There would be no additional copayment for Gary to be recertified and continue to get hospice care.

    d. Correct. Although the standard hospice benefit period is six months, Medicare will continue to cover a patient's hospice care as long as the hospice physician or the medical director of the hospice facility recertifies the patient to be terminally ill.

4.

    a. Incorrect. The statement is true. Medicare Part A covers in-patient or hospital care (and more).

    b. Incorrect. The statement is true. Medicare Part A provides benefits for hospice care.

    c. Incorrect. The statement is true. Medicare Part A provides physician-ordered rehabilitative care in a skilled nursing facility (SNF). Medicare Part A (hospital insurance) may cover care given in a certified SNF if it's medically necessary to have skilled nursing care.

    d. Correct. The statement is false. Medicare Part A (Hospital Insurance) may cover care given in a certified SNF if it's medically necessary to have skilled nursing care (for example, changing sterile dressings). However, most nursing home care is custodial care (for example, help with bathing or dressing). Medicare doesn't cover custodial care if that's the only care needed.

5.

    a. Incorrect. The statement is true. Medicare Part B (medical insurance) covers doctor and other healthcare providers' services.

    b. Correct. The statement is false. Medicare Part B does cover home healthcare. Medicare Part B does cover outpatient care, durable medical equipment, home healthcare, and some preventive services.

    c. Incorrect. The statement is true. Medicare Part B provides coverage for an annual wellness visit. It covers care to prevent illness (like the flu) or detect it at an early stage when treatment is most effective.

    d. Incorrect. The statement is true. Medicare Part B covers an annual flu shot. It covers care to prevent illness (like the flu) or detect it at an early stage.

6.

    a. Incorrect. The statement is true. Medicare Part C or Medicare Advantage plans generally operate as PPOs and HMOs.

    b. Incorrect. The statement is true. Medicare Part C or Medicare Advantage plans generally provide their services through network doctors and hospitals.

    c. Incorrect. The statement is true. Many, but not all, Medicare Advantage plans provide prescription drug coverage.

    d. Correct. The statement is false. Medicare Part D (not Part C) is a prescription drug program that dovetails private insurance policies with Medicare coordination. Medicare Part D covers out-patient prescription drugs (with some limitations).

Chapter 8

Knowledge check solutions

1.

    a. Incorrect. Although the Social Security Administration had hoped for solvency over the next 75 years, quantitative analysis makes clear that the system is solvent only until 2034.

    b. Incorrect. Experts expect the annual cost of Social Security benefits (expressed as a share of workers' taxable earnings) to grow to roughly 16.6% in 2038 and then decline slightly before slowly increasing after 2050.

    c. Correct. The Social Security Administration's analysis presumes that the OASDI system will be inadequately funded by 2027–2034.

    d. Incorrect. Although the combined OASDI program continues to fail the long-range test of close actuarial balance, it does satisfy the test for short-range (10-year) financial adequacy. The trustees project that the combined trust fund asset reserves at the beginning of each year will exceed that year's projected cost through 2027.

2.

a. Correct. Eliminating the taxable wage base would be most likely (from among the choices shown) to lower the shortfalls in the Social Security and Medicare systems.

b. Incorrect. Lowering the taxable wage base would reduce FICA tax and increase the shortfall.

c. Incorrect. Repealing the Medicare tax on unearned income would reduce revenues to Medicare and worsen the shortfall.

d. Incorrect. Permitting pharmaceutical companies to charge Medicare enrollees full retail price for prescription drugs would worsen the shortfall, particularly in light of Medicare Part D.

The AICPA publishes *CPA Letter Daily*, a free e-newsletter published each weekday. The newsletter, which covers the 10-12 most important stories in business, finance, and accounting, as well as AICPA information, was created to deliver news to CPAs and others who work with the accounting profession. Besides summarizing media articles, commentaries, and research results, the e-newsletter links to television broadcasts and videos and features reader polls. *CPA Letter Daily*'s editors scan hundreds of publications and websites, selecting the most relevant and important news so you don't have to. The newsletter arrives in your inbox early in the morning. To sign up, visit smartbrief.com/CPA.

Do you need high-quality technical assistance? The AICPA Auditing and Accounting Technical Hotline provides non-authoritative guidance on accounting, auditing, attestation, and compilation and review standards. The hotline can be reached at 877.242.7212.

Learn More

Continuing Professional Education

Thank you for selecting the American Institute of Certified Public Accountants as your continuing professional education provider. We have a diverse offering of CPE courses to help you expand your skillset and develop your competencies. Choose from hundreds of different titles spanning the major subject matter areas relevant to CPAs and CGMAs, including:

- Governmental and not-for-profit accounting, auditing, and updates
- Internal control and fraud
- Audits of employee benefit plans and 401(k) plans
- Individual and corporate tax updates
- A vast array of courses in other areas of accounting and auditing, controllership, management, consulting, taxation, and more!

Get your CPE when and where you want

- Self-study training options that includes on-demand, webcasts, and text formats with superior quality and a broad portfolio of topics, including bundled products like –
  - CPExpress® online learning for immediate access to hundreds of one- to four-credit hour online courses for just-in-time learning at a price that is right
  - Annual Webcast Pass offering live Q&A with experts and unlimited access to the scheduled lineup, all at an incredible discount.
- Staff training programs for audit, tax and preparation, compilation, and review
- Certificate programs offering comprehensive curriculums developed by practicing experts to build fundamental core competencies in specialized topics
- National conferences presented by recognized experts
- Affordable courses on-site at your organization – visit **aicpalearning.org/on-site** for more information.
- Seminars sponsored by your state society and led by top instructors. For a complete list, visit **aicpalearning.org/publicseminar**.

Take control of your career development

The AICPA's Competency and Learning website at **https://competency.aicpa.org** brings together a variety of learning resources and a self-assessment tool, enabling tracking and reporting of progress toward learning goals.

Visit www.AICPAStore.com to browse our CPE selections.

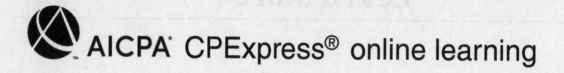

AICPA® CPExpress® online learning

Just-in-time learning at your fingertips 24/7

Where can you get <u>unlimited online access</u> to 600+ credit hours (450+ CPE courses) for one low annual subscription fee?

CPExpress® online learning, the AICPA's comprehensive bundle of online continuing professional education courses for CPAs, offers you immediate access to hundreds of one- to four-credit hour courses. You can choose from a full spectrum of subject areas and knowledge levels to select the specific topic you need when you need it for just-in-time learning.
Access hundreds of courses for one low annual subscription price!

How can CPExpress® online learning help you?

- ✓ Start and finish most CPE courses in as little as 1 to 2 hours with 24/7 access so you can fit CPE into a busy schedule.

- ✓ Quickly brush up or get a brief overview on hundreds of topics when you need it.

- ✓ Create and customize your personal online course catalog for quick access with hot topics at your fingertips.

- ✓ Print CPE certificates on demand to document your training - never miss a CPE reporting deadline.

Quantity Purchases for Firm or Corporate Accounts
If you have 5 or more employees who require training, the firm access option allows you to purchase multiple seats. Plus, you can designate an administrator who will be able to monitor the training progress of each staff member. To learn more about firm access and group pricing, visit aicpalearning.org/cpexpress or call 800.634.6780.

To subscribe, visit **www.AICPAStore.com/cpexpress**

Your strategic learning partner

Let us help prepare your staff for the future.

What is your current approach to learning? One size does not fit all. Your organization is unique, and your approach to learning and competency should be, too. But where do you start? Choose a strategic partner to help you assess competencies and gaps, design a customized learning plan, and measure and maximize the ROI of your learning and development initiatives.

We offer a wide variety of learning programs for finance professionals at every stage of their career.

AICPA Learning resources can help you:
- Create a learning culture to attract and retain talent
- Enrich staff competency and stay current on changing regulations
- Sharpen your competitive edge
- Capitalize on emerging opportunities
- Meet your goals and positively impact your bottom line
- Address CPE/CPD compliance

Flexible learning options include:
- On-site training
- Conferences
- Webcasts
- Certificate programs
- Online self-study
- Publications

An investment in learning can directly impact your bottom line. Contact an AICPA learning consultant to begin your professional development planning.

Call: 800.634.6780, option 1
Email: AICPALearning@aicpa.org